Help,
I'm Knee-Deep in Clutter!

Help,
I'm Knee-Deep in Clutter!

Conquer the Chaos and Get Organized Once and for All

JOYCE I. ANDERSON

AMACOM

American Management Association
New York • Atlanta • Brussels • Chicago • Mexico City • San Francisco
Shanghai • Tokyo • Toronto • Washington, D.C.

Special discounts on bulk quantities of AMACOM books are
available to corporations, professional associations, and other
organizations. For details, contact Special Sales Department,
AMACOM, a division of American Management Association,
1601 Broadway, New York, NY 10019.
Tel: 212-903-8316. Fax: 212-903-8083.
E-mail: specialsls@amanet.org
Website: www.amacombooks.org/go/specialsales
To view all AMACOM titles go to: www.amacombooks.org

This publication is designed to provide accurate and authoritative
information in regard to the subject matter covered. It is sold with the
understanding that the publisher is not engaged in rendering legal,
accounting, or other professional service. If legal advice or other expert
assistance is required, the services of a competent professional person
should be sought.

Library of Congress Cataloging-in-Publication Data

Anderson, Joyce I.
      Help, I'm knee-deep in clutter! : conquer the chaos and get organized once and for
all / Joyce I. Anderson.
           p.   cm.
      Includes bibliographical references and index.
      ISBN-10: 0-8144-7420-9
      ISBN-13: 978-0-8144-7420-4
      1. Storage in the home.   2. Housekeeping.   3. Home economics.   I. Title.

TX309.A63   2007
648'.8—dc22

                                                                        2006025180

Printing number

10 9 8 7 6 5 4 3 2 1

CONTENTS

INTRODUCTION

A magazine writer asked a famous actress, "What's your secret for having such a great figure?" I think you know what the actress said: "I'm careful about not overeating, I use portion control, and I exercise a lot." Well, shoot. We all knew that. Just didn't want to hear it.

The writer was disappointed, too. She had wanted to hear that there was a pill or some kind of magic wand that would let her eat anything she wanted and only have to do a little teeny bit of exercise. However, she knew deep down it was never going to be that easy.

Sorry, but there's no big secret for becoming more organized either. I don't have a magic wand for you to wave and say, "Clutter be gone." What I do have are some steps, tips, and routines to help you control clutter.

The truth is that we're always going to have some kind of clutter. There are two types: totally-out-of-control clutter and plain old normal controllable clutter.

What's uncontrollable clutter? I guess we all know what that is. You've absolutely, completely lost it—it's a monster mess! If your basement is stacked to the ceiling with junk, you know you're not going to be able to fix it up in a few hours. This has become a dreaded PROJECT!

What's normal, controllable clutter? It's the stuff that you can take care of pretty quickly. Maybe you painted the bedroom or just finished a big gardening project and dropped everything off in the basement. You've been extra busy lately and three weeks later the pile is still sitting right where you left it.

If you're basically organized then you know exactly where the paint supplies or the gardening tools belong. You can do a quick fix-up in twenty minutes or at most an hour because you have a system in place.

Everybody's got a combination of controllable and uncontrollable clutter. Your basement might be a mess but your paperwork is very organized, or perhaps your basement looks great but you've lost control of your clothes or the kitchen countertop.

Don't tell yourself that you have to turn it all into a perfect house. You can only have perfection if you're willing to spend hours and hours cleaning and straightening every day or if you have your own cook, housekeeper, personal secretary, and gardener. While you're dreaming, let's just add an upstairs maid and a chauffeur.

Since that's probably not going to happen, ease up on yourself. Instead of yearning for perfection, aim for a comfortable, attractive, and reasonably organized home.

You selected this book to help you. You've got the dream. You're ready to make some changes. I've got the plan to make it easier for you. My goal is to help you eliminate uncontrollable clutter and then figure out easy routines for living with normal, manageable clutter.

Let's take that first step together!

ACKNOWLEDGMENTS

Special thanks to my sister Denice Anderson for her encouragement and proofreading expertise.

I also wish to acknowledge the invaluable assistance of my friends: Katy Haviland, Dottie Symons, Mary Christensen, Susan Zuk, Susan McDonald, Jean Moran, and Steve Morse.

Help,

I'm Knee-Deep in Clutter!

Part One

KNEE-DEEP CLUTTER AND CHAOS

Help! I don't want to do it!

Maybe you're ready to make some changes but you still think you don't have the time or energy to spend organizing and straightening every day. You just kind of let things pile up.

I understand that. I got way off track just after Christmas. I was extra busy. Then when I had some time, I didn't have any energy. Maybe I was coming down after a Christmas cookie sugar high. Anyway, I just didn't feel like doing anything.

I ended up with huge piles of mail that I hadn't checked, and my TO DO folders were overflowing. I lost control of my clothes, and the Christmas decorations were in a heap in the basement. I knew I was going to have to get to them eventually, but each day I kept putting it off.

When you use the "Let-It-Pile-Up System," you feel like you're giving yourself a little break, but what really happens is that you create a lot more work for yourself.

Piles of bills lying around? You start losing track of those bills and important papers and end up paying late fees.

Dishes stacking up? You might have to use tools to chip off the dried food.

Big clothes pile? Just two words: underwear crisis!

Neglected yard? When you finally get around to it, it's like hacking through a jungle.

The "Let-It-Pile-Up System" just makes more work for you. That's why I like to control clutter and chaos with "Daily and Weekly Routines."

I've asked some of my highly organized friends, "How do you keep your homes so nice and neat?" They all said the same thing. It was important for them to have an attractive and organized home, but it was more important to have time for their family, their friends, their work, and activities that they enjoyed.

In order to have more personal time, they followed some routines. First, they figured out that they could cut down on a lot of clutter if they didn't create clutter in the first place. So, they automatically straighten things throughout the day. Second, they have a system for fixing up uncontrollable clutter. Third, they follow quick routines for squeezing in daily and weekly chores, such as paying bills and cleaning the house and taking care of the laundry and dry-cleaning.

That's what works for me, too. How did I get back on track from my Christmas clutter?

- First, I checked my calendar and scheduled a couple of evenings and a Saturday afternoon.

- Next, I started getting organized. During two evenings, I turned on the TV, sorted the mail, and caught up on bills and paperwork. On Saturday, I put away the clothes and Christmas decorations while listening to the afternoon opera.

- Finally, I got back on my "Daily and Weekly Routines" for conquering clutter and chaos. Each day, I dropped the mail off in one spot and put my clothes away immediately. Each week, I tackled some of those bills before they became unmanageable piles.

How about you? Are you ready to begin making some changes? Let's start turning unmanageable clutter into manageable clutter.

Chapter 1

TIME WISE

Help!

Do the events in your life keep jumping up and catching you by surprise? Is the idea of planning ahead an alien concept? Is that why it's midnight and you're making brownies for your son's school party tomorrow? Can you do something about it? You bet! Here's the plan.

The First Part of the Plan Is *Schedule It*

Do you need to schedule a little time to think about ways to, well, schedule your time? Setting up a daily calendar will help. For example:

- You probably can set up your calendar in one afternoon or evening. Pick a time and just do it.
- If you're pressed for time, you can watch TV while you're gathering miscellaneous papers or figuring out what to add to your WEEKLY PRIORITY LIST.

The Next Part of the Plan Is *Organize It*

The following six steps will help you control your clutter.

1st Step: Paper Roundup

PAPER PILEUP

Little pieces of paper can get lost or turn into mysterious piles. Let's get them all together and find out if there's anything worth keeping:

- Start by gathering all your lists, calendars, refrigerator message board, and electronic gadgets. Sort through the information and goggle at the unnecessary duplication.
- Get rid of notes and lists that are old or no longer valid or that already have been added to your calendar.
- In your roundup of clutter culprits, you might discover some receipts, bills, and a friend's new phone number. Put them in one of your business folders and deal with them later.

2nd Step: Master List

THE WISH LIST

The MASTER LIST is a giant wish list of projects and activities that you should do or that you'd really love to do, but, it's not going to happen this month and probably not even this year. Who knows? Maybe someday?

- Set up a TO DO folder for all your lists of things that need to be done. File it by your calendar. If you prefer, set up your TO DO lists on the computer.
- Instead of one long list of things to do, break it down into three categories. For example:
  - BUSINESS: Make a will, increase insurance.
  - HOUSEHOLD: Build a deck, paint bathroom cabinets.
  - PERSONAL: Sort through Mom and Dad's boxes of photos, take golf lessons, learn Chinese.

3rd Step: Yearly Checklist

WHAT? AGAIN?

A yearly checklist can help you see at a glance what fun projects are waiting for you. It also can help make scheduling tasks a little easier:

- Use the detailed YEARLY CHECKLIST in Chapter 23 to help you set up a list in your TO DO folder or on the computer.
- Add all the things that pop up every year, such as birthdays, anniversaries, due dates for taxes and insurance, spring and fall gardening projects, and regular piano tune-ups.
- You also can schedule specific household projects, such as taking time in January to update your address book and washing the carpets in June and December.

4th Step: Weekly Priority List

FIRST THINGS FIRST

If your niece calls and asks for some copies of your Christmas photos, how can you make sure that you won't totally forget about it? If you're like me, you've got to write it down. You need a place to jot things down that you definitely plan to do ASAP:

- Grab a sheet of paper, write WEEKLY PRIORITY LIST at the top, and keep it with the rest of your lists in the TO DO folder.
- Now you won't forget to pick up copies of photos for your niece. It's on the list.
- Instead of one long list of things to do, break it down into three categories. For example:
  - BUSINESS: Start taxes.
  - HOUSEHOLD: Check car maintenance schedule and make appointment.
  - PERSONAL: Get copies of Christmas pictures for Chris, check prices for soccer team t-shirts, call Jaime and Kelsi about lunch plans, get John's new address.

5th Step: Daily Calendar

DAY PLANNER

At the very least you need a daily calendar to keep track of all the things you have to do, such as keeping a dentist appointment and getting the car fixed. Don't forget to add birthdays, meetings, parties, and hockey games:

- ✐ Choose whatever works for you. Use a wall calendar, a desktop book calendar, a computer program, or other electronic devices.
- ✐ If you have a family, it's probably more useful to have something everyone can easily check, such as a prominent wall calendar. Keep a pencil attached.
- ✐ Encourage everyone to always list his or her appointments on this calendar.
- ✐ Since you can't take a wall calendar with you, quickly transfer some of the information onto the calendar that you keep in your purse or briefcase.

THE ULTIMATE CALENDAR

A typical calendar just says that you have a dentist appointment on Wednesday the 5th at 4:30 p.m. and that there's a wedding on Saturday the 22nd at 2 p.m. However, jotting down a little extra information and a few reminders on your calendar can really help you keep on top of things and avoid a lot of last-minute scrambling. It also cuts down on those pesky pieces of paper.

A more useful calendar will look like this:

November

4		Shop for wedding gift this week
5	4:30 p.m.	Dentist—ask about a mouth guard
7		Get clothes, tickets, binoculars ready for tomorrow
8	5:00 p.m.	Leave for dinner—take tickets and binoculars
	6:00 p.m.	Dinner in Greek Town
	8:00 p.m.	Fisher Theater—*Chicago*
21		Get directions, gift, camera, and clothes ready for wedding
		Buy extra film, wash car, and get gas
22	12:45 p.m.	Leave for wedding—take gift, directions, camera, film
	2:00 p.m.	Jan and Ron's wedding
24		Buy groceries for Thanksgiving
25		Make pies

26		Make veggie tray and dip
27	12:15 p.m.	Leave for dinner—take pies, veggie tray, and dip
	1:00 p.m.	Thanksgiving dinner at Mom and Dad's

With this expanded version you won't be getting ready for the wedding and suddenly find that your suit or dress needs to be pressed, that you can't find the directions, or that you're out of film.

6th Step: Sunday Setup

ADVANCED PLANNING

Stop for a minute each week and take a look at your life. What are your commitments for the upcoming week? What else needs to be done around the house?

- Take a few minutes every Sunday and set up your calendar for the week.
- List all appointments, meetings, and extra reminders of things to take or things to do.
- Check your WEEKLY PRIORITY LIST and the YEARLY CHECKLIST. Are there any deadlines?
- Plan on scheduling first things first. For example:
  - If you need to start on taxes this week, don't decide to clean out the garage, too.
  - Your parents are visiting this weekend. You need to get those new pictures into the photo albums.
  - The library book sale is next week. Better start sorting books to be donated.
  - Oh boy, it's time to mulch.
- Check your purse or wallet. Do you have the cash, checks, and credit cards that you need to start the week?
- Prepare your shopping list for the week.

What's the Final Step?

Once you have your calendar and WEEKLY PRIORITY LIST set up, you'll have a lot smoother sailing throughout the week.

Now it's time to *Set Up a Routine to Control Clutter and Chaos.*

DAILY: Take 10 to 15 Minutes

❑ As soon as you get home, check your pockets, purse, or tote bag for notes and receipts.

❑ Put the receipts in a RECEIPTS envelope and add appointments, activities, or future plans to your calendar and WEEKLY PRIOR- ITY LIST. Now toss out all those little pieces of paper.

❑ Later take a couple of minutes to check your calendar and to get out papers and items that you'll need the next day.

WEEKLY: Take 10 to 15 Minutes

❑ On Sunday, pop a chicken in the oven then take a few minutes with the Sunday Setup to figure out all the fun things that are a "must-do" for the week ahead.

❑ What's cookin' this week? Prepare your grocery list.

❑ Is this the week that you might be able to start one of those big projects? Check your YEARLY CHECKLIST and MASTER LIST.

Chapter 2

CORRAL THE BIGGEST CLUTTER CULPRITS

Help!

Once in awhile, for graduation or Christmas parties, your house is in tiptop shape. It sparkles. Then before you know it, it's right back to its usual chaos. You're trying to figure it out: "What the heck happened? Why do I keep having all this clutter and chaos?"

I can answer that. The mess keeps building back up again because you don't have a routine for controlling normal clutter. Can you do something about it? Yes, indeed! Here's the plan.

The First Part of the Plan Is *Schedule It*

OK. You're going after the routine clutter culprits that just keep cropping up. Check your calendar and figure out how you can fit this project into your busy schedule. For example:

- Perhaps you could set up an In-and-Out Shelf Tuesday after work and round up toys on Thursday after dinner.

✐ You probably could finish the following steps in a couple of hours over the weekend.

The Next Part of the Plan Is *Organize It*

The following five steps will help you corral clutter.

1st Step: In-and-Out Shelf

STOP CLUTTER AT THE DOOR

Instead of leaving a trail of jackets and gloves, schoolbooks, and papers throughout the house, set up a drop spot for everything as you first come in the door.

The Setup

✐ Set up an In-and-Out Shelf on a shelf, small table, desk, stool, or bench by the back door.

✐ If you live in a condo or apartment and don't have a back door, place a basket or tray on the kitchen counter.

Clutter Roundup

✐ Incoming items:

• Hang up your coat and drop off all work papers, school items, and new purchases on the In-and-Out Shelf. Drop your purse on the kitchen counter or desk where you sort mail. Take groceries immediately to the kitchen.

• Later, when you're ready to tackle some business papers or look at your new clothes, you'll know right where to find them.

✐ Outgoing items:

• Each night put work and school items back on the In-and-Out Shelf.

• Place film to be developed and letters to be mailed in a basket or tray on the shelf.

2nd Step: Mail and Paperwork

THE PAPER TRAIL

You don't have time to pay bills or plow through papers every day. You just need a place to park your clutter culprits until you're ready to deal with them. Plus, if you keep them all in one spot, you can cut back on frantic searches for misplaced statements and receipts.

The Setup

- ✐ Set up one spot on the kitchen counter, a desk, or a bookshelf as a drop site for all current mail, notes, and receipts.
- ✐ Set up an office area and choose one spot for all important papers and bills to be paid.
- ✐ Set up spots to stack current magazines, newspapers, and catalogs.

Clutter Roundup

- ✐ Zip around the house and put all mail, receipts, and stray pieces of paper in a big box.
- ✐ Find a place for that box in your newly designated office area.

There may be an awful lot of stuff in that box, but now your house isn't littered with papers. (We'll deal with these papers in Chapter 14.)

3rd Step: Clothes

OUTFITTERS

Are there nearly as many clothes on the floor and covering the furniture as there are hanging in the closet? Clothes are not floor decor. Let's get them back where they belong.

The Setup

- ✐ If it will help, place a clothes hamper for dirty clothes in each bedroom.

Clutter Roundup

- ✐ Check out each room and pick up all the clothes.
- ✐ Either hang them up, put them in drawers, or toss them in the laundry bin.

4th Step: Food and Dishes

KITCHEN

Do you have little snack stations all over the house? Everything food-related belongs in the kitchen.

The Setup

- Set up some bags or boxes for items to be recycled.

Clutter Roundup

- Check every room and take all cans, bags of chips, and dirty dishes to the kitchen and recycling area.

5th Step: Toys and Games

THE FUN HOUSE

Is your house a big toy store with toys and games piled up in every room? Set up a couple of specific spots for stacking kid stuff.

The Setup

- Set up a shelf for games and put a large basket or box for toys in each child's bedroom.
- Set up a games shelf and toy basket in your family room.

Clutter Roundup

- Check out each room, scoop the toys and games up off the floor, and return them either to your child's bedroom or to the family room.

What's the Final Step?

Your house is looking pretty good. You still might have some clutter culprits lying around but you've turned your messy, cluttered place into a neat, comfortable, and attractive home. However, here's the age-old question: How long will it last?

You have a system in place for storing daily papers, clothes, food, and toys. Encourage your family to help cut down on these clutter culprits by following a quick daily routine.

Now it's time to *Set Up a Routine to Control Clutter and Chaos*.

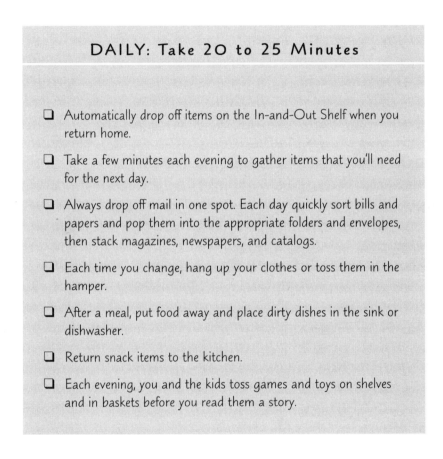

DAILY: Take 20 to 25 Minutes

- ❑ Automatically drop off items on the In-and-Out Shelf when you return home.

- ❑ Take a few minutes each evening to gather items that you'll need for the next day.

- ❑ Always drop off mail in one spot. Each day quickly sort bills and papers and pop them into the appropriate folders and envelopes, then stack magazines, newspapers, and catalogs.

- ❑ Each time you change, hang up your clothes or toss them in the hamper.

- ❑ After a meal, put food away and place dirty dishes in the sink or dishwasher.

- ❑ Return snack items to the kitchen.

- ❑ Each evening, you and the kids toss games and toys on shelves and in baskets before you read them a story.

Part Two

HIP-DEEP
CLUTTER AND CHAOS

What kind of help do you need?

Oh, oh. You're thinking about tackling the tough stuff, the monster messes. You can't get the car in the garage for the fourth year in a row, the kids' bedrooms are way out of control, and your kitchen has no charm, just plenty of clutter. These are the heavy-duty areas that you've been avoiding for years.

It's time to look through the following chapters and pick a project. The basement, your clothes, or paperwork may seem like impossible tasks but they're not. Take a deep breath and then take the first step. Just concentrate on one step at a time and before you know it you'll have tackled a tough project and come out the winner!

Chapter 3

BASEMENT

Help!

You're heading down to the basement. It's kind of like *A Journey to the Center of the Earth*. Who knows what's buried there? To find out, you'll need to do some major digging through your clutter culprits. The main problem is that you don't have a clue how to get started. Can you do something about it? No doubt about it! Here's the plan.

The First Part of the Plan Is *Schedule It*

How busy is this week? Pick one area of the basement to fix up, such as the workshop. Block off some time on your calendar to take on this project. For example:

- Schedule an hour after work on Monday and also on Wednesday to clear out the workshop area.
- Spend three hours on Saturday to clean and organize the workshop.

The Next Part of the Plan Is *Organize It*

The following eight steps will help you control your clutter.

1st Step: The Plan

SPECIAL AREAS

Don't just wade in and start flinging things around. You need a plan!

- Divide the basement into several sections, such as the laundry area and the workshop. Maybe you'd also like to set up a TV lounge, a play area for the kids, or a spot for exercising. It is easier to work with "function" areas because by understanding the purpose of each, you know exactly what belongs there and what doesn't.

- As you work on these areas, unfortunately you'll end up with some pretty impressive piles of things. How do you figure out what to do with them? Flip to Chapter 4 to help you decide where to store everything.

2nd Step: The Fun House in the Basement

RELAX

Concentrate on setting up an entertainment area. Don't get distracted and also start sorting tools and gardening equipment:

- Choose a section of the basement for lounging, partying, and watching TV.
- Pull everything out and set aside.
- Dust the ceiling and shelves and sweep or vacuum the floor. Wash if greasy or grimy.
- Clump items on the shelves. For example, store the CDs together, the tape cassettes on one shelf, and the DVDs and videocassettes on another shelf. Stack all the glasses, plates, and napkins together.
- Set up the lounge area and include items on the list below:
  - Small refrigerator
  - Cart, bar, or shelves for refreshments

- Glassware, plates, silverware, and napkins
- Snacks and beverages
- Bottle opener and corkscrew
- TV, VCR, DVD, CD and cassette player, radio, and remotes
- Videotapes, DVDs, CDs, and tape cassettes
- Ping-Pong table, paddles, and balls
- Pool table, cue sticks, and balls
- Dart board and darts
- Card table and chairs
- Sofa and chairs
- Blankets and pillows
- Lamps and rug
- Tissues and wastebasket

3rd Step: Laundry Area

CLEAN UP

Don't start rummaging through the holiday items and kitchenware. Stick to the laundry and cleaning-related items:

- Pull everything out of the laundry area and set it aside.
- Dust the ceiling and shelves and sweep the floor. Wash if necessary.
- Clump items on the shelves. For example, store the laundry supplies on one shelf and the household cleaning supplies together on another shelf.
- Set up the laundry area and include the items listed below:
  - Washing machine and dryer
  - Basket for dirty clothes
  - Laundry supplies
  - Household cleaning supplies
  - Recycling bins or baskets for bottles, cans, newspapers, magazines, and catalogs
  - Broom, dust pan, mop, pail, and wastebasket

4th Step: One-Stop Shopping

BUY OUT

Ignore all the other fun stuff in your basement. Just concentrate on setting up your pantry area:

✐ Choose a section of the basement for a pantry.

✐ Pull everything out and set aside.

✐ Dust the ceiling and shelves and sweep the floor. Vacuum and wash as necessary.

✐ Cluster items on the shelves. For example, store your extra canned goods together on one shelf and place the extra paper products together on a different shelf.

✐ Set up the pantry area and include:

  • Canned and boxed food
  • Cooking and baking supplies
  • Bags of potatoes, apples, and oranges
  • Snack shelf for chips, pretzels, crackers, and candy
  • Bottled water, soft drinks, beer, and wine
  • Paper supplies, such as toilet paper, tissues, paper towels, and freezer bags
  • Pet food and extra kitty litter

5th Step: Playhouse

RECESS

Forget about all the clothes and gardening items lying around. Focus only on a play area for the kids:

✐ Choose a section of the basement just for the little ones.

✐ Pull everything out and set aside.

✐ Dust the ceiling, wash the shelves, and sweep and mop the floor.

✐ Clump items on the shelves. For example, stack the reading books on one shelf and the coloring books and drawing paper on another shelf. Put all the crayons in a plastic box.

✐ Set up the play area and include the following:

  • Rug and floor cushions
  • Children's table and chairs
  • Small chalkboard and chalk
  • Shelves or plastic boxes for drawing paper, coloring books, and crayons
  • Painting supplies, stickers, and crafts
  • Pens, pencils, children's scissors, ruler, and glue

- Bookshelf with a selection of children's books, games, and puzzles
- Big toy box with a selection of toys
- Puppet theater and rocking horse
- Tissues and wastebasket

6th Step: Shape Up
MUSCLE BUILDER

Concentrate on the exercise area. Don't get distracted by auto supplies and games:

- Choose a section of the basement for your own home gym.
- Pull everything out and set aside.
- Dust the ceiling and shelves and sweep and mop the floor.
- Clump things. For example, store your exercise videotapes on one shelf. Have workout clothes, towel, and shoes in a gym bag ready for heading out to your aerobics class or to play racquetball.
- Set up the exercise area and include:
  - Rug or mat
  - Workout clothes, shoes, towels, and gym bag
  - Punching bag, jump rope, weights, bench, exercise bike, treadmill, steps, rowing machine, and any other equipment you own
  - TV/VCR with exercise tapes
  - Large mirror
  - Tissues and wastebasket

7th Step: Office or Study Hall
THINK TANK

Whether this space is for you to pay household bills, or for the children to do their homework, it will require much the same kind of organization.

Stick to just the office area. Leave the linens and tools for another time:

- Choose a section of the basement for setting up an office.
- Pull everything out and set aside.
- Dust the ceiling and shelves and vacuum, sweep, or mop the floor.
- Clump things. For example, place the extra packs of lined paper and notebooks together. Keep envelopes, stamps, and stationery

together. Stack the box of hanging folders, manila folders, and large manila envelopes that you use to get and stay organized.

✐ Set up the office area and include:
- Desk with lamp, office supplies, and wastebasket
- Extra office supplies
- File cabinets for household, business, and personal papers
- Business papers for your job
- School and college papers
- School and college yearbooks
- Magazines to keep
- Magazine and newspaper articles to save

If you're setting up shared computer/homework space for the children here, instead of or in addition to an office for yourself, you will want to read the section on schoolwork in Chapter 7. Check Chapter 13 for details about organizing a home office for your business.

8th Step: Tool Time
WORKSHOP
Organize your tools and maintenance items. Don't get distracted by the camping and barbecue supplies:

✐ Choose a section of the basement for your workshop.

✐ Pull everything out and set aside.

✐ Dust the ceiling and shelves and sweep the floor.

✐ Clump things. For example, keep regular light bulbs in a box and use a plastic bag to store special ceiling, lamp, or outdoor bulbs. Store all the house-painting items together.

✐ Set up the maintenance and workshop area and include the following:
- Extension cords, light bulbs, and batteries
- Repair and fix-it items, such as glue, sandpaper, caulk, and tape
- Decorating supplies, such as paint, paint brushes, and tarps
- Hardware supplies, such as nails, nuts and bolts, and picture hangers
- Hand-held tools, such as hammers, screwdrivers, and clippers

- Power tools, such as saws and drills
- Manuals and instruction sheets for tools and their maintenance
- Stack of empty boxes
- Toolbox, tool belt, protective goggles, and work gloves
- Workbench, ladder, and stepstool

What's the Final Step?

Great start, but you're not finished yet! You've still got all kinds of miscellaneous boxes and piles to sort through, and if your basement is large enough, you might like to set up some other areas for sewing, crafts, an art studio, a dance floor, a recording studio, or a photography lab.

Keep plugging away and get these areas in shape, then move on to Chapter 4, which has tips to help you finish the basement, attic, and garage and to *Set Up a Routine to Control Clutter and Chaos*.

Chapter 4

BASEMENT, ATTIC, AND GARAGE

Help!

You've pulled all kinds of household items from the laundry, exercise, and pantry areas. Also, don't forget all those other storage shelves packed with junk. Oh, sorry. I mean your treasured personal possessions.

When you have so many clutter culprits, how can you decide where to put everything? You can't just go in and start flinging things around your basement, attic, and garage. Can you do something about it? Certainly! Here's the plan.

The First Part of the Plan Is *Schedule It*

Double-check your calendar and find a few spare hours each week to start sifting through your clutter. For example:

- Maybe you can organize holiday ornaments one day after dinner and coordinate sports equipment on the weekend.

🖎 Next week tackle the kitchen equipment after work and the gardening tools on Saturday.

The Next Part of the Plan Is *Organize It*

The following six steps will help you control your clutter.

1st Step: Storage

BOX 'EM, RACK 'EM, AND STACK 'EM

One of the secrets of organizing is having plenty of boxes and shelves for storage:

🖎 You may have to break down and buy some shelving for your basement, attic, and garage. Fortunately, there are lots of affordable, heavy-duty plastic shelves that you can choose from—and no tools required to assemble!

🖎 You also may need to run out for some inexpensive cardboard or plastic storage boxes. However, don't fill large boxes so full that you can't lift them.

🖎 Put a label on each box. This will make a big difference when you're looking for the Crock-Pot that you only use twice a year.

🖎 Don't forget to label items that are stored in large bags.

🖎 Try to get as many things as you can up off the floor, especially if there's a chance of water getting into your basement, attic, or garage.

2nd Step: Clear the Clutter

PACK RATS

If you can't bear to throw anything away, you need to get yourself psyched up. Take a few minutes to think about getting rid of things. When you're ready to organize the basement, attic, and garage, start on one side and work around the room. Either leave items where they are or put them in one of the following piles:

- Definitely Dump: broken, empty, toxic, faded, stained, smelly
- Recycle: old magazines, newspapers, catalogs, cardboard, cans, bottles, batteries
- Donate: items to offer to family, friends, churches, Kiwanis, Purple Heart, Salvation Army, or thrift shops
- Money-Makers: items for a garage sale, consignment stores, or e-Bay

GET PSYCHED

The more stuff you have, the more hectic your life becomes. How can you decide if it's worth buying or keeping?

- If there was a flood would you try to save it?
- After a fire would you replace it?
- Is it beautiful or useful?
- Tempted to buy a lot while traveling? First ask yourself if you can actually use it or if it fits your home decor.
- If you're sorting through items from a deceased family member, you don't need to keep everything just because it was important to that person. Pull out a few items to display and treasure.

3rd Step: Fun Stuff

THE BIG DECISION

Maybe you want to store the holiday items in the attic, tuck away the outdoor recreation items in the garage, and leave crafts items in the basement. You might decide that the bikes and skateboards should be together near the front of the garage, and the tent and camping supplies on the back shelves:

- To get ready, take everything off the shelves you plan to use and set aside.
- Dust the ceiling and shelves and sweep the floor.
- Now you're ready to put everything back on the shelves. Clump things. For example, store the crafts items together and stack the boxes of games together.

✐ Suggested categories to clump are listed below:
- CRAFTS, including hobby, sewing, and art supplies
- EQUIPMENT, including old VCRs, tape cassette recorders, and radios
- GAMES, including adult board games, puzzles, and playing cards
- HOLIDAYS, including special boxes or shelves for each holiday and separate boxes for outdoor lights and decorations
- OUTDOOR RECREATION, including picnic supplies, camping and hiking items, and hunting and fishing equipment
- PHOTOGRAPHY, including camcorders, cameras, and photo supplies
- SPORTS, including ball box for basketballs and softballs, golf clubs, Ping-Pong set, baseball bats and gloves, and Frisbees
- SUMMER RECREATION, including roller blades, skateboards, and bikes
- SWIMMING AND BOATING, including floating tubes, mats and chairs, wading pool, life jackets, and paddles
- WINTER RECREATION, including ice skates, skis, and sleds

4th Step: Hearth and Home

THE BIG DECISION

First decide: Would it be more convenient to store the extra furniture and decorative items in the attic, the gardening and outdoor things in the garage, and then everything else in the basement?

✐ After you've decided, think about how you want to organize the shelves you will be using. Perhaps you can put the automotive and gardening supplies near the front of the garage and the out-of-season blankets and luggage on the shelves in the back of the basement.

✐ To get ready, take everything off the shelves you plan to use and set aside.

✐ Dust the ceiling and shelves and sweep the floor.

✐ Clump things. For example, store the automotive products together and keep the kitchen items together.

✐ Suggested categories to clump:
- AUTOMOTIVE, including oil, windshield solvent, and cleaning products

- DECORATIVE, including baskets, candles, pillows, and vases
- FURNITURE, including extra chairs, card table, lamps, and paintings
- GARDENING, including rake, hoe, shovel, fertilizer, and insect spray
- HOUSEHOLD EQUIPMENT, including fireplace equipment, fans, and lanterns
- KITCHEN, including large pans, extra glassware, and ice cream maker
- LINENS, including extra comforters, pillows, and quilts
- LUGGAGE, including suitcases, fanny packs, and special travel items
- OUTDOOR FURNITURE, including deck and patio furniture and grill implements
- OUTDOOR MAINTENANCE, including snow shovels, snow blower, lawn mower, leaf blower, and pool maintenance supplies
- PETS, including cages and pet travel carriers, bags of leashes and collars, and grooming supplies

5th Step: Kiddie Corner

THE BIG DECISION

If you don't have an attic or garage then there's no decision. Everything pretty much stays in the basement. Whichever you choose:

- Choose a section of shelves just for the children's items.
- To get ready, take everything off the shelves you plan to use and set aside.
- Dust the ceiling and shelves and sweep the floor.
- Clump things. For example, store the arts and crafts in one area and keep the kids' computer games together in another.
- Suggested categories to clump:
  - ARTS AND CRAFTS, including jewelry kits and painting supplies
  - COMPUTER GAMES, including Nintendo and Play Station
  - DOLLS, including cloth dolls and Ken and Barbie dolls
  - GAMES, including Monopoly and other board games and playing cards

- STUFFED ANIMALS, including Beanie Babies and pandas
- TOYS, including Slinkys, building blocks, and puzzles

6th Step: Let's Get Personal

THE BIG DECISION

If you have an attic, that might be the perfect spot for storing mementos. If not, set up an area in the basement for mementos and extra or off-season clothes:

- Choose the specific shelves for your mementos and a spot for clothes storage.
- To get ready, take everything off the shelves you plan to use and set aside.
- Dust the ceiling and shelves and sweep the floor.
- Clump things. For example, keep the clothes together in one area and store the boxes of mementos on the same shelf.
- Suggested categories to clump:
  - CLOTHES, including off-season daily clothes; special-occasion clothes, such as a tuxedo, evening gown, and wedding dress; clothes for different weight ranges; baby clothes; and clothes for specific sports or seasons, such as swimming suits, water thongs, ski outfits, and hiking boots
  - MEMENTOS, including childhood items saved for yourself, photograph albums, vacation and travel treasures, and items earmarked for your children or grandchildren (tag the items)

What's the Final Step?

Your basement, attic, and garage finally are finished. You're taking your family and friends on tours to show them how great everything looks. How can you keep these areas organized? Now it's time to *Set Up a Routine to Control Clutter and Chaos*.

DAILY: Take 3 or 4 Minutes

❑ Looking for a screwdriver? Don't fling things around and create a mess while you search.

❑ When you're finished with the screwdriver, pliers, or hammer, put each tool back where it belongs.

WEEKLY: Take 15 to 20 Minutes

❑ Doing your regular housecleaning? When needed, tack on another twenty minutes for a little straightening in the basement or garage.

❑ Toss in a load of laundry. Take fifteen minutes to put the new golf balls, detergent, and extension cord in their special spots.

❑ While the roast is in the oven, quickly sweep the garage and straighten up the gardening supplies.

Chapter 5

BATHROOMS AND LINEN CLOSET

Help!

Do your guests, especially the ladies, become rather distant after a glimpse of your bathroom? Is your linen closet overflowing? Maybe it's time to make a few changes. Can you do something about it? Of course! Here's the plan.

The First Part of the Plan Is *Schedule It*

If you're ready to fix up the linen closet, look over your calendar and choose a convenient afternoon. For example:

- After singing in the shower, sing along with the radio or CD player as you sort towels, sheets, and shampoo.
- Set aside another afternoon or evening to organize all your beauty products.

The Next Part of the Plan Is *Organize It*

The following four steps will help you control your clutter.

1st Step: Clump Everything

GET IT TOGETHER

There's not much beauty in most bathroom items. Let's hide them:

- Clump them inside the cabinet, drawers, and cupboards.
- Clump items that go together:
    - BODY CARE, including deodorant and body lotions
    - DENTAL CARE, including toothbrushes and dental floss
    - EYE CARE, including contact lens solutions and eye drops
    - FACE CARE, including soaps, moisturizers, and shaving supplies
    - HAIR-CARE EQUIPMENT, including brush and hair blower
    - HAIR-CARE PRODUCTS, including hair spray and styling gels
    - PERSONAL CARE, including feminine hygiene products

2nd Step: Let's Get Organized

FINE TUNING

Make your bathroom a pleasant little place:

- Add a clock to keep you on time in the morning.
- Set up a radio or CD player for company.
- Store magazines in a small stand.

STORAGE

You can never have enough storage space. Create more storage areas:

- Stack a few extra towels in a basket or on wicker shelves.
- If necessary, install hooks or racks for towels and bathrobes.
- Buy inexpensive open shelves or add a freestanding shelving unit over the commode.
- Add baskets, trays, or racks inside cupboards.
- Store bathroom cleaning products in a plastic pail under the sink or in the linen closet.

✏ If you don't have a clothes chute, get a hamper or basket for dirty clothes.

KID CARE

Make the bathroom kid-friendly but easy to keep tidy:

✏ Add a paper cup dispenser.

✏ Pick a special spot for toothbrushes and towels for each child.

✏ Set up a hanging string bag or basket for bath toys.

3rd Step: The Beauty Counter

MAKEUP STATION

Set up one place (and only one place), such as in the bathroom or your bedroom, for putting on makeup:

✏ Use a small desktop mirror for closeups and keep a box of tissues and a wastebasket handy.

✏ Set up a tray or box for only the cosmetics that you use every day.

✏ Clump the lipsticks together and the eye shadows together.

✏ Stand up eyeliner, mascara, and lip liner in a small container.

✏ Place evening and exotic glittering and gleaming makeup in a small box or cosmetic bag and leave in a drawer or the linen closet until a special occasion arises.

✏ Display colognes and perfumes on the countertop or on an open shelf.

✏ Put small items, such as nail clippers, tweezers, and small scissors in a tray or bowl on a bathroom shelf or in a drawer.

Have teenage girls? Set up makeup stations in their bedrooms so everyone else will have a chance in the bathroom.

BATHROOM BEAUTIFICATION

Look through some of your decorating magazines for ideas:

✏ Cut the clutter on the counter. Keep only permanent items, such as tissues, soap dispenser, hand lotion, a tray for perfumes, a radio or CD player, and a decorative item.

✐ Here are some of the things you could add or change:
- New towels, curtains, rug, and shower curtain
- Matching soap dispenser and toothbrush holder
- New picture and artificial flower arrangement
- Wicker towel stand and new wastebasket
- Large mirror and different light fixtures
- Paint or wallpaper for walls and shutters
- Can of room freshener or fragrance plug-in

BATHING BEAUTY

You might not be able to afford a fancy spa weekend but you can create a spa atmosphere right in your own bathroom:

✐ Use a shower caddy to organize the body wash, shampoo, rinse, and razor that are used every day.

✐ Keep a few specialty body washes, fragrant moisturizers, and a loofah along the back rim of the tub or in a basket. Store the rest in the linen closet.

✐ Treat yourself to a bathtub caddy that has room for a book and a snack.

✐ Get even more comfy with a bathtub mat and pillow.

✐ Perhaps you'd like to keep a little supply of candles and matches to help set the mood for a long, relaxing soak in the tub.

✐ Keep various herbal bath oils and add aromatherapy to match your mood.

✐ Find a nice warm winter robe with a hood to snuggle into after you get out of the bathtub. Look for an attractive and cool summer robe or kimono.

4th Step: Linen Closet

LINE UP THE LINENS

When you open the doors of your overstuffed linen closet, do towels and sheets squish out?

A little sorting can solve that problem:

✐ Clump items together:
- BLANKETS, including comforters and throws

- SHEETS, including separate piles for each size and color
- TOWELS, including separate piles for each style and color

PERSONALLY SPEAKING

The linen closet is your friend. It's supposed to keep all your supplies nice and handy. Don't let it become a dumping ground for clutter culprits.

- Clump extra products:
  - FACIAL AND BODY-CARE ITEMS, including moisturizers and deodorants
  - HAIR-CARE PRODUCTS, including shampoos and conditioners
  - MISCELLANEOUS ITEMS, including cotton puffs and ear swabs
  - PAPER PRODUCTS, including tissues and toilet paper
  - PERSONAL-CARE ITEMS, including feminine hygiene products and birth-control items
- Clump in gallon-size plastic freezer bags or small plastic boxes:
  - DENTAL-CARE ITEMS, including extra toothbrushes and dental floss
  - EYE-CARE ITEMS, including contact lens solutions and eye drops
  - FOOT-CARE ITEMS, including moleskin and corn pads
  - HEALTH-CARE ITEMS, including bandages, cough syrup, and ointments

Check Chapter 12 for more details about organizing health products.

PRETTY AS A PICTURE

Organize all the extra makeup so that it won't be rolling off the shelves:

- Clump your cosmetics in small makeup bags or plastic freezer bags.
- Clump together:
  - EYE-CARE ITEMS, including eyebrow pencils and mascara
  - FOUNDATION, including both liquid and powder, and rouge
  - LIP-CARE ITEMS, including lipstick and lip liners
  - MISCELLANEOUS ITEMS, including makeup brushes and sponges
  - NAIL-CARE ITEMS, including clippers and nail polish

CLEANUP

It's bad enough that it's cleanup time, so don't make it worse by having to run up and down the stairs searching for cleaning supplies. Get them together:

- Keep a plastic pail with bathroom cleaning supplies under the sink or in the linen closet.
- Only fill the pail with supplies you actually clean with—throw out products you no longer use, even if their containers aren't empty.

What's the Final Step?

Your bathroom and linen closet are looking really spiffy. Let's figure out how to keep out the clutter. Now it's time to *Set Up a Routine to Control Clutter and Chaos*.

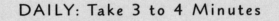

DAILY: Take 3 to 4 Minutes

- ☐ Either hang up towels or place them in the laundry basket.
- ☐ You use your toothbrush, moisturizer, and hair blower every day. Now that you have a special spot for everything, automatically toss things back where they belong.

WEEKLY: Take 5 to 15 Minutes

- ☐ While you're cleaning, spruce up the countertop a little and straighten a messy shelf.

❑ Fill up the liquid soap, put in a new razor blade, and grab some more cotton puffs out of the linen closet.

❑ Make your shopping list. Don't take a chance on running out of TP.

Chapter 6

BEDROOMS

Help!

It would be great to reclaim your bedroom for sleeping and relaxing. Right now there's so much junk and chaos it's giving you nightmares. Can you do something about it? Most definitely! Here's the plan.

The First Part of the Plan Is *Schedule It*

What's your week looking like? Can you find a little time to transform your bedroom? For example:

- If you have a bedroom TV, spend a couple of evenings reorganizing while keeping an eye on your favorite prime-time programs.
- Turn on the radio for a ball game or the opera and finish up the project on Saturday afternoon.

The Next Part of the Plan Is *Organize It*

The following five steps will help you control your clutter.

1st Step: Clearinghouse

CLOTHING TIME

Clothes usually cause the most clutter in bedrooms so they deserve their own special chapter. Plan on tackling your clothes as a separate project when you get to Chapter 8. For now, do the following:

- Don't try to organize your clothes for this project. Just get them out of sight.
- Hang up clothes, put them in drawers, or toss them in the clothes hamper.
- Always keep the closet doors and dresser drawers closed.

EYESORES

It's funny how we can walk right by piles of junk and clutter culprits and not really notice them:

- Stand in your doorway and take a look around. Pull out the sports equipment, jackets, and other items that don't belong in a bedroom.
- Get rid of the ski poles, piles of kids' toys, baskets of clean clothes, shopping bags with new purchases, mail, sales receipts, and dirty dishes. Park them where they belong.

2nd Step: Sleep Aids

TRANQUILLITY BASE

Turn your bed into a comfy refuge. Keep the following items at the side of your bed:

- Telephone and emergency phone list
- Flashlight
- Clock radio with alarm

- Tissues and wastebasket
- Hand lotion, lip balm, cough drops, and nasal spray
- A pair of socks and an afghan
- Books and magazines to read
- Reading glasses
- Paper and pencil for late-night brilliant ideas
- Backrest or larger pillow
- Sleep eyeshades
- Small tape cassette and CD player
- Small collection of tapes and CDs
- TV remote control

You may need to change your nightstand from a simple table to one that has a drawer and shelves in order to accommodate these useful items.

HEALTH NUT

You can sleep more soundly if you organize your bedroom and make it a safer and healthier room:

- Be sniffle free:
  - Regularly dust and vacuum.
  - Take out the extra books and plants (they're major dust catchers).
  - Use polyester bedding rather than feathers or goose down.
- Purchase a pillow to support your neck and a body pillow.
- Hang a smoke detector in the hall outside of the bedrooms.
- Store a folding window ladder in the closet for a second-floor escape in case of fire.

DREAMLAND

Since you spend nearly a third of your day in the bedroom, make it as pleasant a place as possible. Consider incorporating some or all of the following:

- A good reading light and books can be your print version of a sleeping pill.

- If you have the room, add a cozy chair for curling up with a book.
- Catch all the TV news earlier in the day, not just before you turn in. Bad news hardly puts you into the mood to snooze.
- Block out clutter by closing all closet doors and dresser drawers.
- Put in a ceiling fan.
- Use light cotton sheets for the summer and toasty flannels for the winter.
- Store extra blankets in a chest or on a stand at the end of your bed.
- If necessary, make your mattress more comfortable by adding a foam mat.

3rd Step: Sanctuary

THE BOUDOIR

It's kind of hard to get into a mellow mood if you're in the middle of a dump site. Designate your bedroom as a romantic zone:

- Keep a selection of some of your favorite music.
- Set up lighting so that you can adjust for a softer look.
- Buy some attractive sheets.
- Plan for privacy with shades, curtains, and a lock on the door.
- If you have any particular romantic items or reading materials, keep them handy but discreetly out of sight.

LOOKING GOOD

Check Chapter 5 for more details about handling cosmetics. In the meantime:

- Decide if it's more convenient to put on your makeup at a desk or table in your bedroom rather than in the bathroom.
- Keep the cosmetics in a decorative container, or better yet, keep them in a small box or basket that you can store out of sight.
- Check yourself out in a full-length mirror before leaving the house.

4th Step: Decorate

BEAUTIFY YOUR BEDROOM

Home-decorating magazines never photograph a bedroom with clothes, personal items, and other clutter culprits draped over bedposts or on the floor:

- Keep your bedroom clean, simple, and neat.
- Rearrange the room or shift the bed to a different angle.
- Tuck electrical cords out of sight.
- Consider pepping things up by adding some of the following:
  - Matching pillows and a throw rug
  - Lamp and table
  - Pictures or photos

5th Step: Office Work

BUSINESS

If possible, keep your office out of the bedroom. However, if there's no other option then make the best of it:

- Add an attractive desk, chair, and lamp.
- Buy matching desktop organizers and place a decorative item on the corner of the desk.
- Angle the desk attractively across the back of the room.
- Use a folding screen to hide the work area.

What's the Final Step?

Your bedroom is ready for sweet dreams. Let's keep it that way. Now it's time to *Set Up a Routine to Control Clutter and Chaos*.

DAILY: Take 4 or 5 Minutes

❑ No PJ's, undies, or party clothes clutter. Either hang them up or toss them in the hamper.

❑ Make the bed and toss on decorative pillows.

WEEKLY: Take 10 to 15 Minutes

❑ Laundry baskets scattered around the bedroom are not decorative items. Put freshly laundered clothes away.

❑ During your regular weekly cleaning, tidy the cosmetics, dresser top, and nightstand, and remove items that don't belong there.

❑ Replenish tissues and lip balm.

Chapter 7

BEDROOMS — KIDS'

~~~~~~~~~~~~~~~~~~~~~~~~~~~~~~~~

Help!

Your kids' bedrooms are out of control. Clutter culprits have run amok! You've run out of ideas, patience, and hope. Can you do something about it? Well, you can try! Here's the plan.

The First Part of the Plan Is *Schedule It*

Would it work better to clean up their bedrooms Tuesday morning while the youngsters are in school or on a Saturday afternoon while they're out playing? For example:

- The best-case scenario would be you and your child laughing and singing as, together, you clean, organize, and decorate the bedroom. Then you get a big hug and, "You're the best mom ever. I love you."

- OK. Let's go to Plan B. Your children might react a little better if you just make a few changes each week. Let the changes kind of sneak up on them.

✐ If the room is totally out of control, schedule a couple of evenings and become a Zamboni. Just do a clean sweep through the entire room.

The Next Part of the Plan Is *Organize It*

The following five steps will help you control your clutter.

1st Step: Cleanup Campaign

DUMP TRUCK
It's time to tackle the kids' rooms. Take a deep breath, open the door, and wade in:

✐ With or without their help, haul out the sports equipment and other items that definitely don't need to be in a bedroom.

✐ Retrieve any music, movies, and magazines that belong with the family collection.

✐ Pull out dirty dishes, food, and trash.

✐ Put clothes back on hangers or in drawers and place dirty clothes in a hamper. Check Chapter 8 for tips about organizing clothes and accessories.

BREAK TIME
If you set up some attractive shelves, bins, and baskets, their toys and treasures might actually end up in these nice storage areas instead of on the floor:

✐ Use baskets, plastic boxes, or stackable bins for stuffed animals and toys.

✐ Clump the following items on shelves or in baskets:
  • Books and magazines
  • Coloring books, crayons, and colored pencils
  • Crafts items, including paint, beads, and stickers

- Games
- CDs, tape cassettes, videotapes, and DVDs

🖎 Provide a table and chairs for playing games and for working on crafts projects.

🖎 Set up a bulletin board and a small chalkboard.

🖎 Add special shelves to display dolls, stuffed animals, toy airplanes and cars, and trophies.

🖎 Every couple of months rotate toys and games. Put some of them in a bag in the basement. Bring up another bag and provide a fresh supply of fun stuff.

2nd Step: Sleepytime

SNOOZING

Children usually hate to go to bed. Get into the wonderful habit of reading a story each night to the little ones. Encourage the older kids to read for a while before they go to sleep:

🖎 Keep the following handy next to the bed:
- Clock radio with an alarm
- Tissues and wastebasket
- Lamp
- Flashlight
- Book
- Pencil and paper

🖎 Plug in a nightlight for the tots.

3rd Step: Grooming

LOOKING GOOD

Encourage the girls, and especially your teens, to dress and apply makeup in their rooms. This cuts down on them tying up the bathroom:

🖎 Provide a full-length mirror. Set up a makeup station with a desk-top mirror and one box for all your daughter's makeup. Check Chapter 5 for more details about cosmetics.

🖎 If necessary, place a hamper or basket for dirty clothes in each room.

4th Step: Schoolwork

STUDY HALL

Every student needs a quiet place for reading, for doing homework, or for just a little daydreaming:

- Set up a study area with a desk or table and a freestanding or wall-mounted shelving unit.
- Provide a comfortable chair, lamp, and wastebasket.
- Stash a big supply of lined paper, notebooks, folders, pens, pencils, ruler, scissors, and paper clips in the desk or on a shelf.
- Provide a computer and printer with supplies, including computer paper, extra ink cartridges, and blank disks.
- File a dictionary, thesaurus, almanac, and atlas on a special reference shelf over or next to the desk.
- Put up a bulletin board.
- Set up one shelf for all school items, such as schoolbooks, notebooks, papers, library books, and book bag.

5th Step: Decorate

THE PERSONAL TOUCH

Talk with your children and get their ideas about how they'd like to fix up their rooms. If they help decorate and turn their rooms into special places, they might take better care of them. Consider implementing some of the following ideas:

- Painting the walls
- Stencils
- Putting posters or pictures on the walls
- Hanging up paintings done by the child
- Pasting glow-in-the-dark stars on the ceiling
- Sprucing up with a new comforter, curtains, and a throw rug
- Adding big pillows and a beanbag chair for comfortable lounging
- Installing an extra wall shelf or two just for decorative items or that special collection

What's the Final Step?

Wow! The kids' bedrooms are looking great. So what will they be like a week from now? Try to get your youngsters to follow these simple routines. Now it's time to *Set Up a Routine to Control Clutter and Chaos*.

DAILY: Take 5 to 10 Minutes

❑ If you had previously given up on hospital corners, at least have them pull up the sheets and comforter after they get out of bed.

❑ Every time they change clothes, either hang them up or toss them in the hamper.

❑ All food and dishes must be returned to the kitchen.

❑ Take a couple of minutes each night to drop toys in the basket, place games on a shelf, and stack CDs, books, and papers.

❑ Take a couple of minutes every evening to gather up all school items for the next day.

WEEKLY: Take 10 to 15 Minutes

❑ Swing through their bedrooms each week and do a quick pickup, check for clutter culprits under the bed, and then dust and vacuum.

❑ Take a couple of minutes to straighten the underwear drawer or reorganize books and papers that were used for a big school report.

Chapter 8

CLOTHES AND ACCESSORIES

Help!

You love clothes and beautiful accessories. Your closets and dresser drawers are bursting with clutter culprits. That makes it hard to find a specific blouse or slacks, and when you finally spot the item it's in a wrinkled-up pile or squashed in between more wrinkled and jammed-in clothes.

Your philosophy always has been that you can never have too many clothes. It might be time to rethink that. Can you do something about it? Yes. Right this minute! Here's the plan.

The First Part of the Plan Is *Schedule It*

Is spring or fall around the corner? The change of seasons is a perfect time to prune your clothes tree. For example:

- Pick a day or weekend and get all your clothes and closets in shape.

- Turn on some music and strut your stuff with a little fashion show.

- If you don't have a lot of time or energy, spread it out. One evening sort through your jewelry while watching TV and on another day tackle the coat closet after work.

The Next Part of the Plan Is *Organize It*

The following seven steps will help you control your clutter.

1st Step: Space-Savers

FILL 'EM UP

Do you need to run out and buy a few closet organizers or plastic boxes?

- Hang blouses, shirts, skirts, and pants on multitiered hangers.
- Use clear flat plastic boxes for storing sweaters under the bed.
- Place shoes in stackable shelves or in a hanging compartment bag.
- Hang belts, ties, and scarves on racks.
- Set up a rack for hanging necklaces.
- Arrange jewelry in a jewelry box.
- Drop off items that you frequently wear, such as a watch, rings, earrings, and cuff links, in a small tray or bowl on your dresser.

THE LINEUP

Even the smallest changes can help your clothes situation. You'll be able to spot what you need faster, and your clothes won't get so wrinkled:

- Hang clothes so that they're all facing the same way.
- If you only have wire hangers, consider switching to plastic ones.
- Place shoes with the heels facing out. Exception: Protect special evening shoes by leaving them in their boxes.

◷ If you don't have space to line up shoes, keep them in their boxes with the labels facing the front.

◷ Line up handbags in a box or square basket.

2nd Step: Get Rid of It, Sell It, or Give It Away

WEEDING THE COLLECTION

You open your closet and it's your wardrobe, your "collection." You've personally selected almost every item. How can you possibly part with one single pair of capri pants? It might not be as hard as you think. Here's what to do:

◷ Get a stack of bags or boxes and set up piles for items to dump, recycle, donate, or sell.

◷ Start on one side of your closet, pull out your first item, and try it on. Don't forget to check out that rear view. You don't need it if it doesn't make you look your best. Work your way from one side of the closet to the other side.

◷ Clothes out—let them go if:
  • "Whoa. What was I thinking?"
  • There's no oomph. If it doesn't do anything for you, if it's dowdy and not your color, dump it.
  • You haven't worn it in years and still wouldn't even if it came back into fashion.
  • Your lingerie or PJ's and robe are stained, frayed, or faded.
  • Shirts, slacks, jackets, or coats are badly stained or damaged.
  • It doesn't fit your current lifestyle for work, leisure, sports, or special occasions. For instance, it's way, way too short or revealing.
  • Ask yourself, "Is it flattering? Do I love it? Is this the image I want to project?"

◷ Steppin' out—let shoes go if:
  • They're just plain ugly.
  • They pinch your toes or scrape your heels.
  • The heels are too high. You'd be in agony just walking to the car.
  • They have broken straps, run-down heels, and aren't worth repairing.
  • They no longer go with any of your outfits.

✐ Accessories—let them go if:
  • You have pierced ears, pull out the killer clip-ons.
  • You have a lot of old costume jewelry that you don't like anymore.
  • You just have too much. Question how many earrings, gold chains, pins, bracelets, cuff links, and tie clips you actually use or really need.
  • There are too many scarves, ties, and belts that aren't flattering or don't match any of your clothes.
  • You have frayed scarves and hats and tattered or single gloves that you can do without.

3rd Step: Seasonal Setup

THE FOUR SEASONS

How can you arrange your collection so that you can find things more quickly?

✐ Divide your wardrobe by seasons. If your closet is large enough, put fall and winter clothes on one side and spring and summer clothes on the other side.

✐ If necessary, use a spare closet or a rod and garment bags in the basement or attic for storing off-season clothes.

OUTERWEAR

Check the coat closet or coat rack by the back door. Do you have your very own discount coat store? Are you tripping over shoes and boots?

✐ Once again, pull out the off-season items and store them elsewhere. This will make room for the things that you're actually wearing, such as jackets and trench coats during the warmer months and bulkier coats during the winter.

✐ Set up a shelf or box for all gloves, hats, and scarves.

✐ Get some inexpensive shelving units for stacking winter boots, hiking shoes, and the like.

4th Step: Get It Together

DEGREES OF SEPARATION

Your frazzle meter goes way up each morning if your jeans, business suits, sweatpants, and dresses are all mixed up together:

⌇ At the very least, have your work clothes separated from your sweats and jeans.

⌇ Set up a separate section for each of these types of clothing and accessories. You could even get fancy and have different-color plastic hangers for each section.

⌇ Here are some examples of how to group clothing and accessories:
  - ACCESSORIES, including belts, scarves, ties, jewelry, hats, and handbags
  - CASUAL AND WORK CLOTHES, including slacks, sports coats, pant suits, skirts and jackets, and dresses and sweaters for a relaxed workday and for dining out and visiting friends
  - FOOTWEAR, including dress shoes, heels, flats, loafers, sandals, thongs, deck shoes, sports shoes, and slippers
  - FORMAL WORK CLOTHES, including business suits, pant suits, jackets, and dresses
  - LEISURE AND SPORTS, including jeans, sweatpants, polo and t-shirts, shorts, and exercise and sportswear
  - LINGERIE AND NIGHTWEAR, including underpants, briefs, bras, slips, socks, nylons, pajamas, fancy PJ's, nightgowns, and robes

⌇ Separate storage is best for the following items:
  - EVENING AND SPECIAL-EVENTS CLOTHES, including suits, tuxedo, gowns, and uniforms
  - WEIGHT-FLUCTUATION CLOTHES, including clothes you used to wear when you were heavier or thinner

5th Step: Color Coordination

COLORIZE

If you're really in an organizational mood, go all the way and arrange clothes by color:

⌇ Put the black slacks together, the navy slacks together, and the red tops together.

⌇ Fold and stack sweaters by color.

⌇ Sort socks so you don't have to squint to see whether you're holding navy or black socks. Stick the white socks in between them.

⌇ Use drawer trays or plastic freezer bags to keep black, gray, and navy nylons separated.

✐ Sort your winter hats, scarves, mittens, and gloves by color. Then you'll be less likely to be in the car and notice that you have on brown gloves with your navy coat.

6th Step: The Family Jewels
THE JEWELRY BOX
When you're in a hurry, you don't want to waste time untangling long necklaces or searching for one missing earring:

✐ Keep the sets of jewelry (pearl necklace and matching earrings, for example) that you wear together each in its own jewelry box.

✐ Sort and separate your general collection of earrings, bracelets, pins, and necklaces.

✐ Give yourself some more room by storing the big orange bead necklace and Christmas tree earrings in a separate box or bag until you need them.

✐ Keep the earrings, ring, and watch that you wear every day in a tray on your dresser.

7th Step: Children Only
KID STUFF
Follow the same plan when setting up closets for your kids:

✐ Mornings might be a little less hectic for everyone if school clothes are all together on one side of the closet and play clothes are on the other side.

✐ Since you usually have to drag teens out of bed each morning, convince them that they can sleep in longer if they get their clothes ready the night before. (Good luck with this one!)

✐ If the problem is dirty clothes on the floor, put a clothes basket in each bedroom.

What's the Final Step?

Your clothes are looking good. How can you keep your collection uncluttered? Now it's time to *Set Up a Routine to Control Clutter and Chaos*.

DAILY: Take 5 Minutes

❑ Every time you change, do the usual: hang 'em up or put 'em in the hamper.

❑ Park clothes in the same place every time you put them away so you can instantly find your red sweater or navy socks.

WEEKLY: Take 30 Minutes to 1 Hour

❑ Wash clothes regularly. Take a TV or computer break to pop clothes into the washer or dryer.

❑ Sort, fold, iron, or sew on buttons while watching TV or listening to the news.

SEASONALLY: Take 2 to 3 Hours

❑ At the end of each season take an afternoon to rotate off-season clothes.

❑ While you are putting away favorites from the season just passed, keep a ferocious eye out for clothes you never wore—not even once—this season. Perhaps it's time to dump, donate, or sell those items instead of letting them take up precious storage space.

❑ Have a fashion show with the upcoming season's clothes: try everything on, and pull out clothes to dump, donate, or sell. (Reread the Second Step from earlier in this chapter before you do this.)

❑ Make a shopping list of items you need in order to update your wardrobe.

Chapter 9

ENTERTAINMENT CENTER

~~~~~~~~~~~~~~

Help!

You're always tripping over stacks of CDs, cassettes, videotapes, DVDs, books, magazines, and newspapers. When you're in the mood to watch *Dumb and Dumber* you don't want to waste a single second searching for it through piles of clutter culprits. Can you do something about it? Lights! Camera! Action! Here's the plan.

The First Part of the Plan Is *Schedule It*

The fun thing about organizing your entertainment items is that you can fix them up while actually listening to music or watching TV. For example:

- Choose an evening, pile up your videos and DVDs, turn on a movie, and start sorting.
- Take another afternoon or evening and fix up your books while watching a ball game.
- Plan on wrapping up the whole project over the weekend.

The Next Part of the Plan Is *Organize It*

The following five steps will help you control your clutter.

1st Step: Entertainment Tonight

TV GUIDE

Hey, when you need your TV remote, you need it. Let's get organized for fun:

- Get a small box or caddy for the TV, DVD, and VCR remotes and the *TV Guide*.
- Curl up in front of the TV with soft blankets and big pillows. Store the blankets in a big wicker basket.
- Rearrange the furniture for good TV viewing. You don't want a lot of glare from the windows.
- Have tables and coasters handy for your snacks and beverages.

THE BIG PICTURE

When you're settling in for a movie, you don't want to waste time sifting through stacks and stacks of videotapes and DVDs:

- Donate movies, educational programs, and children's videos that you know you'll never watch again to schools or to your local Boys and Girls Club.
- If necessary, buy some inexpensive videotape and DVD shelving.
- Arrange videotapes and DVDs:
  - BLANK TAPES: Store in one convenient place.
  - CHILDREN AND TEENS: Set up a special spot for all the Disney movies and teen topics.
  - EDUCATIONAL: File by subject, such as biography, history, and science.
  - FAMILY: File your family vacations, reunions, school athletic events, new baby, and holiday videos separately from your regular videotapes (label all videos that you tape).
  - MOVIES: File alphabetically by title or group them by subject, such as musicals, science fiction, and westerns.
  - RENTALS: File in a special spot.

2nd Step: Musical Moments

FINE TUNING

Before you can sit back and relax with some of your favorite music, you might need to do a little organizing:

- If you have a new CD and also a copy on a tape cassette or record album, consider pulling out the old copy.
- Let it go if you bought it, never liked it, and haven't listened to it since that first time you brought it home.
- If necessary, purchase some CD or tape cassette storage holders.
- Arrange CDs, tape cassettes, and records:
  - BLANK TAPE CASSETTES: Stack together in a convenient spot.
  - CHILDREN'S MUSIC: File on a special shelf.
  - CLASSICAL: File alphabetically by the group, artist, or composer.
  - POPULAR: File alphabetically by the group, artist, or composer.
  - SPECIAL COLLECTIONS: File by types of music, such as classical and country.
  - TEEN MUSIC: File in their rooms.

NOTEWORTHY

It's time to tickle the ivories. Turn those stacks of piano sheet music into a little music library:

- Repair or throw out old piano and guitar sheet music that is torn or has missing pages.
- Keep current sheet music favorites in the piano bench.
- If you have a lot of sheet music, stack it on a shelf, put it in folders, or stand it in plastic storage bins.
- File large music books and piano lesson books on a shelf or in plastic storage bins.
- Arrange sheet music and music books:
  - CHILDREN: File music on a special shelf or in a plastic bin.
  - CLASSICAL: File alphabetically by the composer.
  - PIANO LESSON BOOKS: File by grade level.
  - POPULAR: File alphabetically by song title or by type, such as country and rock.

• SPECIAL BOOK COLLECTIONS: File by categories, such as Broadway and jazz.

3rd Step: Subscriptions

CANCELLATION TIME

Are you wasting money by subscribing to so many world news and financial magazines and newspapers that you can't read half of them?

- ✐ Cut back subscriptions to what you realistically can read each month.
- ✐ If you're tripping over stacks of old magazines and newspapers in the basement, plan on some major recycling.
- ✐ Keep the last year of magazines and donate the rest to friends, to the school library, or to a local senior citizen center.

THE DAILY NEWS

Those pesky clutter culprits. They just keep coming day after day, week after week. What do you do with all the magazines, newspapers, and catalogs?

- ✐ Spread out current magazines on a coffee table or stack them next to your favorite chair.
- ✐ Set up a spot for magazine back issues and articles that you haven't had a chance to read.
- ✐ Stack today's newspapers by your chair. After reading the papers, place them in the recycling bin. If you get behind, stack new papers on top of the previous papers. At the end of the week, quickly skim them and then toss in the recycling bin.

4th Step: The Bookstore

BOOKENDS

You really don't have to keep every single book. It's actually OK to get rid of some of your collection:

- ✐ Consider giving away or dumping some of these books:
  - Those having mildewed, torn, or brown and cracking pages
  - An older edition of the same book

- Old high school or college textbooks that you haven't opened since you left the classroom
- Nonfiction and reference books having outdated information

✐ Save a few favorites and pass on some of the mysteries, romance, and science fiction that you've collected.

IT'S ONLY MAKE BELIEVE

It's handy to have your fiction books organized when you're looking for a specific title to read or to loan to a friend:

✐ Clump fiction books:
- ADULT FICTION: File in alphabetical order by the author or by subject, such as fantasy, mystery, and romance.
- CHILDREN'S BOOKS: Stack on low shelves where children can have easy access.
- SPECIAL COLLECTIONS: File special mystery, science fiction, or rare books separately.
- TEEN FICTION: File in alphabetical order—or just be happy if they're stacked together.

JUST THE FACTS

Set up your own library and file all the nonfiction books together. You don't have to maintain a full-scale reference library; there's always the Internet at home or in the public library:

✐ Clump nonfiction books:
- CHILDREN'S BOOKS: File on low shelves.
- GENERAL SUBJECTS: File by subject, such as biographies, diet, health, movies, and sports.
- OVERSIZE BOOKS: Stack flat in bookshelves or on a coffee table.
- REFERENCE: Set up a shelf for the almanac, atlas, dictionary, and thesaurus.
- SPECIAL COLLECTIONS: File special Civil War, poetry, or rare book collections separately.
- TEEN NONFICTION: File by subject.

READING CORNER

Give yourself, your spouse, and the kids an inviting place to curl up with a good book:

- Set up a comfy chair in the corner with a reading lamp.
- Keep your reading glasses, tissue box, and a wastebasket handy.
- Set up a shelf where you can always find the newest books, as well as books checked out from the library.

5th Step: The Play Station

DISCARD

If you're overwhelmed with piles of toys and games, give yourself some more room by discarding a few items. Dump some family games and computer games:

- Toss games that are in bad shape with missing or broken pieces.
- If you've just bought the new version, pass on the old one.
- Donate games that are too easy or too difficult for your family.
- Get rid of games that are too violent or otherwise inappropriate for your children.

GAME ROOM

Encourage your kids to play some games instead of just parking themselves in front of the TV all the time:

- Keep a card table handy so that you can quickly set it up for playing games or working on a puzzle.
- Arrange games on shelves:
  - CHILDREN'S GAMES: Store some in their bedrooms.
  - COMPUTER GAMES: Store the current favorites near the computer and keep the rest together on a shelf in the basement.
  - EQUIPMENT: Store extra cords, blank disks, and ink cartridges in a box or inside a cabinet.
  - GAMES AND CARDS: File a few games, such as Monopoly, Pictionary, Uno, and playing cards on a shelf in the family room and the rest on a special shelf in the basement.

TOYS ARE US

Your kids don't need to be surrounded by 100 percent of their toys 100 percent of the time:

- Keep some toys and games in their rooms, some in the family room, a few in the basement play area, and the rest out of sight in the basement or in a closet.

- Each month you can retire some of the toys for a while and bring out some others. The younger ones will feel like they are getting new toys, and you won't be wading knee-deep in kid stuff.

- Set up a big box or basket for toys. Take a minute each day and get the children to help you quickly pick up their toys and toss them in the basket.

- Don't forget your furry friends. Keep a small wicker basket full of pet toys.

CRAFTY

Be ready when you feel that creative urge. Keep your crafts and projects handy:

- If you knit or do needlepoint, keep what you need together in a basket or box. Then when you have a few minutes for your cross-stitching or a project, you don't have to wander around getting it all together.

- If you don't have a separate room or spot for crafts projects, set up a corner of the family room or dining room where you can leave your easel and paints or woodworking projects out.

What's the Final Step?

The fun stuff at last is under control. How can you keep it from piling up again? Now it's time to *Set Up a Routine to Control Clutter and Chaos*.

DAILY: Take 5 Minutes

- ❏ You're finished with the CD, computer game, or book. Automatically pop it back where it belongs.

❏ Each evening do a quick pickup. It doesn't have to be perfect. Just get magazines and newspapers off the furniture and floor and onto a shelf.

WEEKLY: Take 10 to 15 Minutes

❏ Before you start your weekly housecleaning, quickly file the clutter culprits.

❏ If necessary, do a little fifteen-minute tweaking and reorganize a messy shelf of CDs or computer games.

ANNUALLY: Take 2 to 3 Hours

❏ Once a year take an afternoon and start sorting your entertainment items. Offer some to family and friends, dump broken items, and donate books you'll never read again, music and movies that you didn't really enjoy, and outdated computer games.

Chapter 10

FOYER, LIVING ROOM, FAMILY ROOM, AND DINING ROOM

∿∿∿∿∿∿∿∿∿∿∿∿∿∿∿

Help!

Lately you've been hip-deep in clutter culprits. Wouldn't it be nice to have attractive and comfortable places where you can entertain friends and where you and your family can relax and enjoy TV, music, games, and nice long naps? Can you do something about it? Yes, you can! Here's the plan.

The First Part of the Plan Is *Schedule It*

The foyer, living room, family room, and dining room are big areas and you've got a lot going on in your life. It might be easier to fix up these rooms if you concentrate on one room at a time, such as the living room. For example:

✐ Choose an afternoon or evening to set up a pleasant area for guests.

✐ Rearrange furniture on Monday, check out your plant situation on Wednesday, and consider adding some room dividers on Thursday.

The Next Part of the Plan Is *Organize It*

The following eight steps will help you control your clutter.

1st Step: Chit-Chat

CONVERSATION PIT
Set up your living room and family room for comfortable conversation:

✐ Shift the furniture so that your guests aren't too close or too far away from each other.

✐ Leave enough space between the sofa and the coffee table or ottoman for people to cross their legs.

✐ Set up convenient places to put drinks and snacks.

✐ Provide a couple of overstuffed pillows for lounging on the floor.

✐ Place comfy pillows, baskets, or blankets at your cat or dog's favorite snoozing sites.

2nd Step: Green Peace

GREEN THUMB
Consider adding more beauty to your home with a few plants:

✐ Place plants together that have the same light requirements.

✐ Place arrangements on shelves, on top of bookshelves, or in clusters on the floor.

✐ Add a tall jar or vase with artificial flowers at the landing on the stairway or in a dull corner spot.

✐ A mixed collection of large and small plants can be a creative room divider.

3rd Step: Feng Shui It

SPACED OUT

Browse through some of your house and garden magazines to get some new decorating ideas:

- ✐ Stand back and look at your room. Is it boxy, with everything lined up square with the walls? If so, you might want to perk it up by angling the sofa and chairs.
- ✐ As in the feng shui philosophy, rearrange furniture so that there is a natural flow through the room and into the next room.
- ✐ You don't want the space to look or feel awkward. Is one side of the room too busy but the other side empty?

ROOM DIVIDERS

You may not be able to afford household renovations, but you can change the look of your home with some room dividers:

- ✐ Folding screens can add a unique decorative touch.
- ✐ Use a bookshelf or several plants to divide an area.
- ✐ Put bookshelves back-to-back in order to separate a room into two distinct areas.
- ✐ Screens and bookshelves can serve as a divider between the living room and the dining room or can block off the view of the bathroom or the basement door.

4th Step: Art Attack

ON DISPLAY

Whether you have *objets d'art* or plain ol' knickknacks, be careful how you place them. Your collection may start looking like clutter if the pieces are all over the place:

- ✐ If you have art objects or are a collector, display your antiques or teacups in special cabinets (save yourself some serious dusting). Consider locked cabinets if you have little kids around. You don't want your treasures broken.

- If you have a lot of photos, don't set them up all around the room. Instead, place them together on a table, piano, fireplace mantel, or bookshelf.

PICTURE THIS

Take a few minutes to decide the most artistic way to display your pictures:

- Be sure that they go with your color scheme and the style of the room.

- Pictures should fit into the available space. Don't hang one little picture all by its lonesome on the longest wall in the room. Also, don't hang a huge picture in a small area.

- Be sure that you don't hang pictures too high on the wall. Your eye level is the rule of thumb.

- Clumping several pictures can be a lovely focal point in your hallway or in your living or dining room. Remember, it's better to have a few nicely placed pictures than cluttered walls.

- There is an exception. A wall totally covered in framed pictures can be spectacular.

5th Step: Accentuate the Positive

HOUSE BEAUTIFUL

Are you thinking about redecorating? Look at the pictures in home style magazines for ideas:

- Spice up the room with some accent pillows, slipcovers, and throw rugs.

- Mirrors over a fireplace or along a stairway can add to the beauty and openness of a room.

- Wastebaskets are a necessity of life so you might as well make them as attractive as possible.

- Use a chest for a coffee table or end table.

- Brass, ceramic, or copper vases are eye-catching and add nice highlights in dark corners.

- Feeling exotic? Add some wicker and bamboo.
- Place a lamp or plant on top of a small stack of books. Make sure to have a saucer under the plant to protect the books from spills. Be very careful when you water.
- Brighten up bookshelves with a picture, plant, or decorative items. Stack some of the books horizontally with the titles facing out for added visual interest.
- What's your window situation? New window treatments can work miracles. Go for a whole new look with blinds or shutters.
- Freshen your home with potpourri, sachets, and scented candles or plug-ins.

6th Step: Lighten Up
TURN IT ON

Check out your lighting sources. Are your overhead lights too harsh and your reading lamp too dim?

- Put three-way bulbs in some of your lamps to provide softer lights for parties or a romantic evening and stronger lights for reading and playing games.
- Try out some of the new bulbs with lower energy use and natural-spectrum lighting.
- Consider floor lamps or track lighting for added effect.
- Spend a little time checking out your cord situation. We don't want to see them! Tuck cords under the lamp base, tape them to the back of a table, roll them up and use a rubber band to hold them together, or buy a cover for cords and cables.
- Scented and votive candles add a lovely glow and welcoming fragrance. Be careful that you don't place them where they could be knocked over, and never leave lit candles unattended!

7th Step: The Welcome Mat
HATS OFF

Keep the foyer and coat closet free of clutter culprits and that jumble of coats, gloves, and boots:

- Buy a set of wooden hangers for guests' coats. Leave space so that coats and jackets won't be crammed into the closet.

- Purchase inexpensive shelves for the top of the coat closet. They're handy for stacking caps, hats, gloves, and scarves.
- Add an interesting coat rack, either standing or on the wall, or maybe an umbrella stand in your entryway.
- If people frequently come in your front door, use an attractive mat or large tray for their wet shoes, boots, and umbrellas.

FIRST IMPRESSION

Welcome people into your home with a warm and inviting entryway:

- Enhance the foyer with a plant, a jar with artificial flowers, pictures, a mirror, a small table and lamp, or a throw rug. Got a grandfather clock around somewhere? Display it here.

8th Step: Fine Dining

TABLE MANNERS

Your mood and digestion will improve if your dining room has a peaceful and attractive atmosphere:

- Keep the dining room table clear. Place one decorative item on the table, such as a floral arrangement, a bowl of fruit, or a set of candlesticks.
- Use a pretty tablecloth or a cloth runner.
- If you have cabinets, display special dish sets and glassware.
- Enhance the area with a picture, throw rug, or plants.
- Buy new curtains or switch to blinds or shutters.

What's the Final Step?

Well, what do you know! You and your family are really enjoying your home. Plus, if guests stop by unexpectedly, your place looks pretty good.

OK. What's the maintenance plan? Now it's time to *Set Up a Routine to Control Clutter and Chaos*.

DAILY: Take 10 to 15 Minutes

❑ Remember: You won't have to pick up clutter if you don't create it in the first place.

❑ Take the blinders off. Don't ignore that jacket, baseball mitt, or screwdriver cluttering the room. Stop, pick it up, and park it where it belongs.

❑ Each evening swing through all these rooms for a quick clutter pickup.

WEEKLY: Take 5 to 20 Minutes

❑ Before you begin your weekly cleaning, take a few minutes to pick up any items cluttering the foyer, living room, family room, and dining room.

❑ Take twenty minutes before one of your favorite TV programs begins and straighten up a few messy spots.

MONTHLY: Take 1 to 2 Hours for Each Project

❑ Every month or so finish your regular housecleaning—then tack on a big project, such as washing the rugs or floor, cleaning windows, potting houseplants, or brushing pet fur off the furniture and curtains.

Chapter 11

KITCHEN

Help!

Do clutter culprits pop out when you open cupboard doors? Is everything either crammed into the cabinets or piled up on the countertop? This isn't the cozy, cheerful kitchen that you'd like for your family. Can you do something about it? Naturally! Here's the plan.

The First Part of the Plan Is *Schedule It*

Are you ready to convert your kitchen into a four-star establishment? For example:

- Maybe sort the canned goods Tuesday after dinner and rearrange the countertop after work on Thursday.
- If you're pressed for time, make it a month-long project. One week concentrate only on cleaning the refrigerator and organizing under the sink. The next week rearrange the canned goods. Continue to do one or two steps each week until you're finished.

⊘ If you have some time off from work, take a day and just tackle the whole kitchen.

The Next Part of the Plan Is *Organize It*

The following eight steps will help you control your clutter.

1st Step: Rack 'em and Stack 'em

RACK 'EM

Browse in your local home-goods stores and consider buying some kitchen organizers and space-savers:

⊘ Add more storage space for your canned goods and boxed items by putting revolving shelves in corner cupboards.

⊘ Double your space with wire racks or plastic storage bins.

STACK 'EM

Organize your canned goods so that you can spot what you need at a glance:

⊘ Line up all items so that the names are facing front.

⊘ Alphabetizing your canned goods sounds a little too much but it's actually pretty helpful. The baked beans and condensed milk are always on the top shelf and the tuna fish is on the bottom. You know right where everything is.

⊘ Always place new cans of soup, diced tomatoes, and other staples in the back and use the older cans first.

⊘ Give yourself the pleasure of opening a cupboard and seeing your own snacks and goodies grocery stored all on one shelf.

⊘ Buy in bulk. Stack the extra cereal, canned goods, soft drinks, and bottled water in a pantry or special storage area in the basement.

2nd Step: Clumping

WHAT'S COOKING?

Let's get those supplies in order. Then when you're all set to make chocolate chip cookies, you won't waste a single second searching for the ingredients:

- ✐ It's a time-saver to store all cooking supplies, such as sugar, flour, and oil, together.

- ✐ Store spices on a rack or in a drawer. Oh, go on. Put them in alphabetical order.

SHAKE AND BAKE

Your baking and cooking utensils keep getting mixed up or shoved out of sight. Arrange them so you can find them right away:

- ✐ Stack the pots and pans together.

- ✐ Consider hanging some pots from a ceiling frame.

- ✐ Arrange the lids by size and store them in the drawer under the oven or in a plastic box.

- ✐ Clump the baking dishes, such as muffin trays and cake and pie pans.

- ✐ Stack baking trays. If possible, slide them vertically into a cupboard or cabinet.

- ✐ Stand cooking utensils, such as spatulas or a large fork and spoon, in a decorative vase or jar. Store the rest of your cooking utensils in a drawer near the stove.

- ✐ Set up another container or drawer for your measuring items, such as cups, spoons, candy and oven thermometers, and weights and measuring chart.

- ✐ Use plastic shoebox-size containers on shelves in cupboards or in your pantry to store items that you only occasionally use, such as a gravy whisk, basting brush, or hand mixer.

SAFETY ZONE

Take a couple of minutes to think about a few kitchen safety precautions:

- Place oven mitts and pot holders in a drawer or hang them on a rack next to the stove.
- Cut down on nicks and cuts by storing knives in knife racks or in cardboard protectors.
- If you have kids, put matches out of sight, and out of reach, in the top cupboard.
- Be sure to have a kitchen fire extinguisher handy. You can mount a small extinguisher on a wall or stand it on the counter.

SERVING AND SAVING

Serving dishes and storing containers can take up a lot of space. A few minutes of organizing will give you more room:

- Clump all casserole dishes, serving bowls, platters, and lids together.
- Put bubble wrap or several layers of paper towels in between special bowls and platters to help avoid chips.
- Place the plastic food containers and the freezer containers together. Keep the lids in a separate plastic box.
- Stack the serving dishes that you don't use regularly on a higher shelf.

PAPER OR PLASTIC?

Are you always rummaging around trying to find the freezer bags or aluminum foil?

- Keep the aluminum foil, food wrap, plastic storage freezer bags, and plastic garbage bags handy in a cupboard or under the kitchen sink.
- Set up a spot for extra table napkins, paper plates, and drinking straws.
- Keep the extra paper towels and other supplies in your pantry or in a special storage area.

3rd Step: The Diner

THE MESS HALL

It's time to set the table. Is it a hassle or is it convenient?

- Stack the flatware, cups, glasses, and dishes so that they are near each other and close to the dishwashing area. It will save you time for setting the table and also for returning items after they've been washed.
- Store flatware in an organizing tray. Keep your special silverware in a protected box or cabinet.
- Keep the napkins and salt and pepper shakers on a lazy Susan or napkin tray on the table, or put them together in a nearby cupboard.
- Stack plastic bowls, cups, and cereal on lower shelves for the younger kids.
- For your thirsty bunch, set up a paper cup dispenser or designate a plastic cup for each person to use for water or soft drinks.
- Coffee cups, mugs, and supplies near the coffeepot will be appreciated when you stumble in for that first cup in the a.m.
- How many place settings, glasses, and mugs do you use regularly? Add a couple more. If you have a bunch left over, store the extras somewhere else, such as in the basement.
- Store glasses by size. Line up the tallest glasses on one side of the cupboard, the medium glasses in the middle section, and the shorter glasses on the other side.
- Place your special sets of dishes and glassware on the top shelves since you use them infrequently. If you have a cabinet, display special items so that you can enjoy seeing them every day.
- Set up a convenient spot to feed your cat or dog. Protect the floor from spilled water and food bits by placing water and food bowls on top of an inexpensive plastic table mat.

4th Step: The Counter Revolution

COUNTERATTACK

Are your appliances taking over? Your coffee maker, toaster, microwave, electric can opener, small TV, and radio have almost completely covered your countertop—and don't forget the bread box and cookie jar:

- Decide which appliances and items you use regularly—several times a week—then move the other ones off the counter. Once you clear out some of the clutter you'll have more work space. Also, it will be easier to clean the area.

- Can you attach the microwave under a cupboard or angle it across a corner?
- Could you add an inexpensive storage shelf or cart for some of the appliances?
- Perhaps a kitchen island could offer room for an appliance or two and add extra work space. It's also a wonderfully inviting spot for family and friends to sit around and enjoy each other's company.
- Place a large plastic cutting board over the sink when you need extra work space.

5th Step: Fixin' Up the Fridge

COLD STORAGE

You're in and out of the refrigerator a dozen times a day. It's important to keep it clean and organized:

- Dump spoiled food, then remove everything else and give the inside of the refrigerator a quick once-over with a damp cloth. Clean off the dried food spots.
- If necessary, defrost the refrigerator while it's empty.
- Put your fruit, vegetables, and condiments back in their special storage areas. If you need to, buy separate plastic containers for fruits and vegetables.
- Make sure that food is covered with a lid, foil, or plastic wrap.
- Put things that you use most frequently on the sides and near the front.
- Adjust shelves for taller items.
- Buy plastic containers for the freezer. Keep poultry, fish, and red meat in separate containers. It cuts down on rummaging around for the fish sticks.
- Decorate the door with magnets or tape up the latest drawing from your six-year-old.
- I personally like to read diet tips posted on the door as I'm reaching for a triple scoop of ice cream.

6th Step: KP Duty

SUDS UP

The fun parts about a kitchen are cooking and eating. Unfortunately, somewhere down the line it's all got to be cleaned up. You might as well make KP duty as convenient as possible:

- Keep all the dish-cleaning products, including dishwashing liquids and granules, sponges, and scrub brushes, close to the sink.
- Store the dish towels, hand towels, dishcloths, and aprons together.
- Install a towel rack inside a cupboard door for hanging damp towels and dishcloths.

MR. CLEAN

It's that time again. Make cleaning a little easier by keeping all your housecleaning items handy:

- Store your kitchen cleansers together under the sink or in a nearby cupboard.
- If you have room, set up a plastic bucket for the products you use regularly each week, such as a dust rag or wipes.
- Keep a separate caddy or plastic bucket for other products that you don't use every week, such as furniture wax, window cleaners, floor wax, and fabric and rug cleaners.
- Don't store any of your cleaning items near food, plates, or cooking utensils.
- If you have small children, store all toxic products out of their reach or behind a locked cupboard door.
- Broom closets are made for the tall items, such as brooms (of course), mops, vacuum cleaner, and ironing board. You also can add a dustpan, pail, and iron. If you don't have a broom closet, set up one special spot so that you can keep these items handy.

RECYCLING CENTER

Are you one of those folks who needs two carts to get all the returnable cans and bottles into the grocery store? Let's get you a new system:

- Set up containers for trash and for recycling.
- Train everybody to do the right thing and pitch items into the recycling bins. Don't leave soft drink bottles, empty cans, or old newspapers lying around.
- Take bottles and cans to the store and other recyclable materials to the recycling center regularly. Don't wait until it takes a forklift just to get them to your car.

7th Step: Using Your Noodle
WORK SPACE

Sitting at the kitchen table is nice, but sometimes you need a work space where you also can leave out some papers and office supplies:

- Find a spot in your kitchen or family room where you could set up a small table or desk in a corner. Store a selection of office supplies for yourself and for the kids to use when they're doing their homework.
- The desk also might work as a family message center for phone messages, shopping lists, and a calendar of scheduled appointments and events. Set up a spot for the mail.
- Add a small plant, a decorative item, or some cartoons and uplifting quotes.
- Keep your recipe box handy with only the recipes that you actually use or have used. Separate them by type of food, such as meat, salads, vegetables, and desserts.
- Leave an envelope or box at your desk or in a cupboard and toss in all the scrumptious recipes that you've torn out of newspapers and magazines but haven't tried yet.
- If you don't have much space, only keep a few of your favorite cookbooks. Store the rest on a bookshelf in another room.
- If there's no room for a desk, perhaps you could set up one corner of the kitchen counter for your telephone, calendar, daily mail, and a desk caddy with pens, pencils, scissors, and a notepad.

8th Step: Perk Up the Place
KITCHEN DECOR

Once everything is organized, it's time to see how you can make it more attractive and cozy:

✎ Look through some decorating magazines for ideas.
✎ Try adding a few of the following items:
  • Fresh flowers
  • Plants or artificial flower arrangements
  • Baskets hanging on the wall
  • New or more pictures on the wall
  • Different curtains
  • Runner or mats on the kitchen table
  • Small centerpiece for the table
  • Bowl of fruit on the counter
  • Decorative canisters
  • New wastebasket
  • Small wind chime
  • Small strand of tiny decorative lights draped across the top of the windows
  • A three-way bulb or dimmer switch to change the lighting for a softer, calming atmosphere while dining and a brighter light for cooking and cleaning
  • A night-light

What's the Final Step?

Your kitchen looks terrific. What's the secret for keeping it organized? Rather than letting dishes grow into a huge pile, put yourself on autopilot and just take a few minutes each day to do minimum KP duty.

Now it's time to *Set Up a Routine to Control Clutter and Chaos*.

DAILY: Take 10 to 15 Minutes

❑ After every meal, quickly put food away, drop dirty dishes in the sink or dishwasher, and wipe up the table, counter, and stove. During the day, take a couple of minutes to put snack items away.

❑ Wipe off a spaghetti splotch or coffee splatter from the cabinet door or wall.

❑ It'll only take a minute or two to place trash and spoiled food from the refrigerator into the garbage pail and to toss bottles and cans into the recycling bins.

❑ Taking the garbage out every night is a hygienic habit to get into—and it keeps odors from greeting you in the morning.

WEEKLY: Take 15 Minutes

❑ Use weekly housecleaning time to clear off any newly cluttered areas on the counter.

❑ Straighten up a messy drawer or a cupboard filled with clutter culprits while you're waiting for the meatloaf to cook.

❑ Take fifteen minutes before the evening news begins and wash the floor.

ANNUALLY: Take 2 to 4 Hours for Each Project

❑ Once a year wash and wax the cabinet doors.

❑ When you're up for a little spring cleaning, pull everything out, clean the cupboards, and rearrange as needed. Use the steps in this chapter to help you reorganize.

Chapter 12

HEALTH AND SAFETY

∿∿∿∿∿∿∿∿∿∿∿∿∿∿

Help!

After such disasters as 9/11, the tsunami, and Hurricane Katrina, we all talked about getting ourselves organized so that we would be prepared in the event a disaster came our way. Even though our family's health and safety are important to us, most of us still aren't really prepared. We either don't have many first-aid supplies or we have to dig through a jumble of stuff when we need help fast. If there were a medical emergency, many of us wouldn't be able to answer a doctor's questions about our family's medical history. If there were a disaster, we'd be caught empty-handed. Can we do something about it? Let's get prepared. Here's the plan.

The First Part of the Plan Is *Schedule It*

This is an important project that won't be too difficult if we all take it a step at a time. For example:

- Settle in front of the TV, lay out all your daily medications, and then organize them.

✐ On another day, turn on some music while you set up a disaster kit.

The Next Part of the Plan Is *Organize It*

The following six steps will help you organize for your health and safety.

1st Step: Daily Medications

PILL ORGANIZATION

If your medications, or meds, are scrambled together in a box or on a shelf, we can tighten up the system and save some time each day.

Meds Check

✐ Gather up all your daily prescription medications and supplements.

✐ Flush meds that are out-of-date or that you no longer use.

✐ Make a daily meds list of medicine taken at certain times of the day. Check the directions and, if necessary, add some reminders, such as "take a half hour before eating" and "don't take with milk or grapefruit."

Medicine Box

✐ Make separate piles for the morning, afternoon, and evening pill bottles and supplies:

- Line them up in the same order on a kitchen shelf.
- If you prefer, store them in plastic shoebox-type containers. Toss your morning, afternoon, and evening pills in separate plastic freezer bags and keep them in the box along with the daily meds list.

✐ Use another plastic box for extra meds and the spare bottle of vitamins you got on sale.

✐ Don't store medications in the bathroom or near the stove in your kitchen. Heat and humidity can affect them.

⊘ Place all boxes of medications out of the reach of youngsters. Ask for child-proof caps for your prescription medicines.

⊘ However, if you live alone and have trouble opening some of your bottles, ask the pharmacist or a friend to remove the caps for you.

Pill-Poppin' Time

⊘ Check drugstores and large home-goods stores for plastic pill containers. There are lots of choices. You can even use electronic pillboxes that beep to remind you to take the pills and electronic pill dispensers that dole out preprogrammed doses. My, what will they think of next?

⊘ Keep the pill containers next to the boxes of medication.

⊘ Every Sunday set up all medications for the next week. Each morning set out the container for that day and your pills will be ready.

⊘ Have separate sets of containers and personal daily meds lists for each member of the family.

⊘ If you're caring for elderly parents, be sure that they have daily pill containers they can open and daily meds lists they understand.

⊘ Never share your medication with anyone else.

2nd Step: Miscellaneous Meds

MEDICINE CABINET

Now it's time to tackle the ointments, sprays, bandages, and other meds that are scattered around the house. Our goals are to cut down on clutter and to store emergency supplies in one section of the linen closet or on a special shelf.

Out-of-Date

⊘ Gather up all miscellaneous medical supplies. Check the expiration dates and toss the meds that will no longer be effective.

⊘ Dump all the bottles, boxes, and tubes that are empty or if the lid or tube is dried, encrusted, or rusted.

General First Aid

- ✐ Buy four or five plastic shoebox-size containers.
- ✐ The first box might include:
  - Adhesive bandages (assorted sizes), adhesive tape, antiseptic wipes, butterfly bandages, corn pads, cotton roll and balls, cotton-tipped swabs, disposable cold packs, disposable hand wipes, elastic bandages, first-aid manual, gauze bandages (various sizes in pads and rolls), insect repellent, latex gloves, safety pins, scissors, a sling (triangular bandage), sterile nonstick dressings, a thermometer, tongue depressors (for finger splints), and tweezers.
- ✐ The second box might include:
  - Antacids, cold remedies, creams and ointments, diarrhea preparations, headache meds, motion-sickness pills or patches, painkillers, sleeping pills, and sunscreen.
  - Use plastic freezer bags to keep some of these items separate. Then just grab the bag with ointments for cuts, scrapes, and bruises or the bag with creams for itches and rashes depending on your needs.
- ✐ Boo-Boo Box for the small fry might include:
  - Cough syrup, creams and ointments for rashes and scrapes, decorated bandages, ear or rectal thermometer, insect repellent, ipecac, and sunscreen.
- ✐ You may need separate boxes for special health items including:
  - Stockpiles of contact lens solutions and supplies, diabetic supplies, and an inhaler and supplies for asthmatics.
- ✐ Set up a section of a shelf for seldom-used items including:
  - A heating pad, a hot water bottle, an ice bag, old knee braces, and spare eyeglasses in a plastic bag.
- ✐ Pet Care Box in the basement might include:
  - Flea and tick collars or drops, grooming products, heartworm medication, and prescribed medications.

3rd Step: Medical Paperwork

OFFICIAL INFORMATION

Now that all the actual medications are under control, it's time to look into the paper situation.

Better get out your headache tablets (and now you know right where they are). Paperwork really is a pain in the neck, but once it's organized it will be relatively painless to maintain.

Current Information

- Keep track of all medical appointments and concerns on your calendar.

- Drop all medication receipts in an envelope and keep it in the side of your meds box.

- Set up a temporary ACTION folder at your desk for all paperwork involving an operation and stay in the hospital.

- If your physician, hospital personnel, or insurance people have any questions, you can quickly check your calendar, receipts, and ACTION folder.

- Make a list of questions and concerns to take to your next doctor's appointment or trip to the veterinarian's.

- When your teens head off for college, give them their personal and family medical histories and a family emergency phone list.

- If you are caring for aging parents, prepare a family medical fact sheet and personal fact sheet for each parent and give them copies.

PERMANENT BUSINESS AND HOUSEHOLD Folders

- A PERMANENT BUSINESS AND HOUSEHOLD folder for health and medicine includes:

  - A list of all doctors, phone numbers, addresses, and (if you know) when you first contacted them. (See Chapter 16 for information about PERMANENT BUSINESS AND HOUSEHOLD folders.)
  - Lists of past and current medications, which doctor prescribed them, and when they were cancelled (and why).
  - Drug information sheets from the pharmacy that include directions for using each med and possible side effects.
  - A personal medical history for each family member, including blood type, list of immunizations, operations, hospital stays, diagnosed diseases, and chronic health problems.
  - A family medical history, including diseases or health problems for

parents, siblings, grandparents, and aunts and uncles and their ages or cause of death.

✐ PERMANENT BUSINESS AND HOUSEHOLD folders for insurance include:
  • One general insurance folder with policy information for all your policies.
  • Separate insurance folders for auto, dental, home, life, long-term care, medical, and vision.

✐ A PERMANENT BUSINESS AND HOUSEHOLD folder for pets includes:
  • The name, age, and description of each pet along with a photo.
  • The veterinarian's checklist of shots, medications, and health concerns for each pet.

PERSONAL INTEREST Folders

✐ PERSONAL INTEREST folders include:
  • Folders for health articles that you've torn out of magazines and newspapers on topics such as arthritis, cancer, diet, and exercise. (See Chapter 16 for information about PERSONAL INTEREST folders.)

4th Step: Household Safeguards

CHILD-PROOF YOUR HOME

Make sure your house is safe for children.

Bumps and Falls

✐ If you have toddlers, pack the tablecloths away until they're older—they can accidentally pull them off along with a load of plates and food.

✐ Attach gates at the top and bottom of stairs to prevent children from climbing or falling.

✐ Lock windows and never allow children on a balcony or high porch unsupervised.

✐ Check that swings and slides are safely constructed.

✐ Be sure kids wear helmets and knee pads when bike riding and skating.

⊘ Provide an athletic supporter, elbow and knee braces, and protective padding for contact sports, plus sport safety glasses.

Burns and Cuts

⊘ Keep highchairs away from the stove.

⊘ Turn pot and pan handles inward so they can't be bumped or grabbed by children.

⊘ Place matches in a high cupboard.

⊘ Use plastic cups and dishes.

⊘ Keep all sharp objects, such as kitchen knives and workshop tools, out of the reach of children.

⊘ Place scissors and sewing kits in drawers.

⊘ Either remove glass coffee tables until the youngsters are older or put protective covers on the corners.

Water Safety

⊘ Let the phone ring. Never ever leave children alone in the bathtub or around a pool, a small wading pool, buckets of liquid, or even an open toilet—small children can drown in only inches of water.

⊘ Put protective spout covers on bathtub spouts.

⊘ Use life jackets when boating, swimming, and playing on a dock.

General Precautions

⊘ Store all medications where children can't reach them.

⊘ Place cleaners and toxic supplies in a locked area or on a high shelf.

⊘ Some household plants are poisonous—keep them away from the little ones.

⊘ Be watchful when dogs are around. Never leave small children alone with animals.

⊘ Never ever leave an infant or small child alone in a vehicle.

⊘ Don't purchase toys and games that might be dangerous to toddlers.

⊘ Tie up drapery and blind cords; they can be hazardous to kids.

🖉 Store hunting knives and firearms in a lockbox with a double lock.

🖉 Add trigger locks to firearms.

🖉 Lock ammunition in a separate place.

SAFETY PATROL

Look around and see what needs to be organized to safeguard your home.

Burns, Cuts, and Crashes

🖉 Adjust the hot water heater so that it's no higher than 120 degrees Fahrenheit.

🖉 Don't wear long sleeves or lean over the stove burners while cooking.

🖉 Use caution when taking food out of the microwave.

🖉 Slow down and avoid nicks when you're using a razor to shave.

🖉 Be extremely careful whenever using electric saws and drills.

🖉 Always use protective eyeglasses when working in the workshop.

🖉 Prevent falling in the bathtub by putting a nonslip mat or decals in the tub or by adding a safety bar or railing.

🖉 Secure overloaded bookshelves or storage shelves that could tip over.

🖉 Don't hang heavy pictures and mirrors by beds.

🖉 Don't leave clutter on the stairs.

🖉 Replace torn stair carpeting.

🖉 Remove slippery throw rugs.

🖉 Move electrical cords that might cause tripping.

Fire Protection

🖉 Place smoke detectors on each floor, check the batteries each month, and replace the batteries once a year. Many people automatically put in new batteries during the spring or fall time change.

🖉 Keep a fire extinguisher on each floor and be sure all family members know how to use them.

- Remove all fire hazards, such as big stacks of papers, old turpentine, and oily rags.
- Store flammable materials, weed killers, and pesticides away from heat sources.
- Don't leave candles unattended or holiday lights on when you're not home.
- Be sure that the fireplace is cared for properly.

Utilities

- Install a carbon monoxide detector.
- Make sure the teenage and older members of your family know how to turn off the main water, gas, and electricity valves.
- Replace frayed electrical wiring.
- Don't overload electrical sockets.
- Don't use a hair dryer or other electrical appliances near water.
- Get surge protectors for your TV, computer, and microwave.
- Have the furnace serviced every two or three years.

Vehicles

- Keep your car in good working order—regularly check the breaks, headlights, turn signals, and tires.
- Check at the end of the chapter for a detailed list of emergency items to carry in each vehicle.
- Always keep your doors locked.
- Don't leave pets in vehicles.
- Never leave the car running while you pop into the store for just a second.
- Stop smoking in the car; it can cause major health problems for your passengers.
- Don't talk on the phone while you're driving—even with a hands-free earphone set. The distraction can cause an accident.
- Avoid the driving sins of going too fast, too slow, tailgating, unsafe passing, not using turn signals, zigzagging out of your lane, failing to yield, ignoring red lights and stop signs, and blocking an intersection.

In the Yard

- Keep toys and bikes off the porch and driveway.
- Never leave a lit grill or fire pit unattended.
- Surround your pool with a locked fence.
- Be careful when swimming alone and when people have been drinking or are very hot.
- Place a safety pole and flotation device by the pool.
- Don't allow glass objects in the pool area.
- Store pool chemicals in a safe and dry place.
- Have the pool treated weekly to prevent the growth of bacteria.

5th Step: Emergency Planning

PLAN OF ATTACK

We all know how unexpected events can turn a life upside down or destroy it. We can't prevent bad things from happening, but we can do some advanced planning to help us cope with emergencies.

Emergency Communication Plan

- Keep an emergency phone list by each phone and a copy in your purse or wallet:
  - Include the phone numbers for doctors, the Poison Control Center, local emergency rescue services, the location of the nearest hospitals, and family members to contact.
  - Make a list of the names and phone numbers of your children's schools and the names, addresses, and phone numbers of their friends.
- Be sure that each child knows his or her name and address and how and when to dial 911.
- Always wear your medical alert tag.
- Provide all pets with ID tags or microchips that are injected under the animal's skin. The chip contains an ID number and information that can help reunite you with your pet.
- Be sure that the address for your house is clearly visible from the street so that ambulances and firefighters won't have difficulty finding you.

- If there's an emergency, everyone should know several different escape routes out of the house. Do a couple of trial runs each year.
- In case of fire, family members should have a specific place to meet in the neighborhood.
- In case of a disaster, choose another place where you can all meet.
- Make plans to pick up elderly parents and relatives if necessary.
- Choose an out-of-state relative or friend as a contact in case your family is separated during an emergency.
- If you live in an area prone to earthquakes, tornadoes, floods, forest fires, hurricanes, or mudslides, make arrangements to stay with family members who live out of the area in the aftermath of a disaster. Call the Red Cross and find out the location of community shelters in your area.
- Stay tuned to weather and news reports so you can respond quickly if you need to.
- In an emergency help elderly or disabled neighbors. Make plans with neighbors for childcare in case parents can't get home.

Prevent Crime

- Never give out your account numbers, Social Security number, and personal identification number (PIN) to unknown sources on the phone.
- Guard your credit cards—be sure that people behind you at the bank's automatic teller machine (ATM) or in stores can't see your account numbers.
- Always be highly vigilant when alone at an outside ATM.
- Check your bank and credit card statements each month. Call immediately if there are any discrepancies.
- Regularly shred all outdated documents that list credit card information, phone bills, bank statements, and investment information.
- Get an annual credit report from one of these three credit bureaus:
  - Equifax: 800.685.1111
  - Experian: 888.397.3742
  - TransUnion: 800.888.4213

- Hang up on any unknown callers who ask you to send them money or if they ask for personal information, such as credit card or checking account information or your Social Security number.
- Add a deadbolt to all your outside doors as well as an extra patio door lock.
- Consider investing in an alarm system or think about getting a dog.
- If you can't afford a system, just displaying an alarm system decal might be enough to deter a break-in.
- Use dawn-to-dusk or sensor lights to turn on front and back porch lights.
- When you're gone, always keep your doors and windows locked.
- Don't make it easy for thieves to slip into your house while you're out in the yard. If gardening in the front yard, keep the back doors and windows locked. When you're in the pool or relaxing in the backyard, lock the front doors and windows.
- While on vacation make sure your place looks like someone is home. Use automatic timers for the lights, TV, and stereo.
- If you haven't stopped your mail and newspaper deliveries, ask your neighbors to keep an eye on your home and to pick up mail and packages while you're traveling.
- Trim the bushes around your house.
- Lock up ladders.

Fire!

- Make sure everyone in the family knows these fire safety basics:
  - If you're on fire, Stop, Drop, and Roll.
  - If you smell smoke, drop to the floor, cover your mouth and nose, and crawl out.
  - Touch a closed door before you open it. If it's hot, don't open it!
  - If trapped in a room, put rugs, pillows, or blankets up against the door to slow the smoke from coming in. Wait by the window for help.
  - Buy a window chain ladder for exiting from an upstairs window.
  - Never go back into a burning building.
  - Meet family members outside the house by a specific tree or a neighbor's porch.

✐ Keep originals of birth certificates, the mortgage, and important financial and investment information in a bank safe-deposit box.

Emergency Shelter

✐ If there is a tornado warning, a bad thunderstorm, or a blizzard:

- Stay away from windows.
- Set up a safety spot in the safest corner of the basement, under the basement steps, or behind a sofa. Provide some chairs, floor pillows, blankets, magazines, and games.
- Grab the kids and pets, a battery-operated radio, water, snacks, and your purse or wallet and get them settled in.
- Keep your disaster kit nearby in case you're trapped there. Check page 96 for a detailed disaster kit list.

✐ If there is a power outage or you're confined to your home:

- Be sure that the disaster kit has a three-day supply of water and nonperishable food, a battery-operated radio, flashlight, lantern, and extra batteries.
- Keep a corded phone or cell phone on hand. Cordless phones don't work without electricity. (If you've gone to a digital or Internet-based phone service and plug your phone in through a modem, your corded phone will not work either.)
- Make sure family members know how to open the garage door manually.
- Set up a bucket with a lid, plastic bags, and ties for a makeshift toilet along with a supply of toilet paper.
- During a power outage turn off lights and unplug appliances to avoid a power surge when the electricity returns. Leave one light on so you'll know when the electricity is back on.
- Keep the refrigerator door closed as much as possible so your food won't spoil.

Internet Safety

✐ Again, never give out vital information, such as your account numbers, Social Security number, or PIN to unknown sources.

✐ Set up strict computer guidelines with your children—let them know that you frequently will be monitoring their online activities.

🖎 Calmly but firmly remind them of the "stranger danger" involved with giving out their name, phone number, address, and other information to strangers they meet on the Internet.

🖎 Don't play into the hands of online gamblers and hucksters whose only goal is to get your money and disappear.

Medical Emergencies

🖎 Don't hesitate. If there's a possibility that someone is having a heart attack or stroke, has suffered a serious cut, burn, or fall, or has been poisoned, immediately call 911.

🖎 There are lots of pamphlets, books, and first-aid courses available. Learn basic first aid and at least a simplified version of cardiopulmonary resuscitation (CPR).

🖎 In an emergency follow basic first-aid principles. First response includes:

- Check the victim, then act fast if breathing has stopped, there's profuse bleeding, or there's evidence of poisoning.
- If breathing has ceased, administer artificial respiration and CPR.
- Stop any bleeding. Cover the wound with a sterile gauze pad or clean cloth and apply direct pressure. Elevate the wound. Wrap a bandage around the pad of cloth to keep pressure on the wound. If bleeding continues, apply pressure at a pressure point; make the person comfortable and treat symptoms of shock, such as strong thirst, nausea, and vomiting.
- If poisoned by fumes, get the person into fresh air. If poisoned by ingestion, call the Poison Control Center.
- Do not move the person unless his or her life is threatened.
- Do not administer anything by mouth until approved by a doctor.
- Treat for shock. Make the person as comfortable as possible; keep him or her warm but don't overheat; and reassure and quiet the person.
- Send someone for help or yell for help. Call for help continuously while performing the necessary first aid.
- Call your doctor even if the medical emergency seems minor, especially if a baby or elderly person is involved. Keep an emergency phone list by each telephone and in your purse or wallet.

6th Step: Disaster Kit

IT'S TIME TO HIT THE ROAD

We could pack a disaster kit and, if we're lucky, never have to use it. Let's not take a chance—let's be as prepared as we possibly can.

Disaster Kit for Evacuation

✐ Use several camping backpacks, duffel bags, and waterproof coolers on wheels for disaster kits. Keep them handy in a hall closet or at the foot of the basement steps, and in an emergency, just grab them and run. They should be stocked with:

- WATER: Plan on one gallon per person per day. Replace every six months so you'll have fresh water, and include water-purifying agents.
- FOOD: Keep a three-day supply per person of nonperishable foods, such as canned meats, fruits, and vegetables, beef jerky, canned juices, dried soup in a cup, powdered or canned milk, peanut butter, crackers, nuts, trail mix, hard candy, and vitamins along with a manual can opener and a set of plastic or paper cups, plates, and utensils.
- CLOTHING/BEDDING: Have one complete change of clothes and sturdy shoes for each person, hats, gloves, rain gear, blankets, and sleeping bags.
- HEALTH ITEMS: You will need a first-aid kit and manual, a bag with extra prescription medications, extra eyeglasses and sunglasses, dentures, contacts, and a list of medications, family physicians, and special health needs of individual family members.
- BABY CARE: Make sure you have formula, powdered milk, bottles, diapers, sanitary wipes, and plastic bags for soiled diapers.
- TOOLS AND SUPPLIES: These include a battery-powered radio, flashlight and extra batteries, matches, watch or battery-operated clock, utility knife, and sewing kit.
- SANITATION: Don't forget toilet paper, towelettes, soap, liquid detergent, feminine hygiene supplies, and personal hygiene items.

✐ Other necessary items are credit cards, cash, coins, and house and car keys. It's best to have plenty of $1, $5, and $10 bills on hand. During a disaster many people won't give you change back on a purchase.

⬿ Important documents should be kept in a bank safe-deposit box. Originals of the following papers (and copies of those at the bank) should be stored in a waterproof container, including:

- Wills
- Insurance policies
- Deeds and mortgage papers
- Passports
- Social Security cards
- Bank account numbers
- Credit card account information
- Household inventory list
- Important phone numbers
- Birth, marriage, and death certificates

⬿ A supply of books, cards, board games, and hand-held electronic toys, as well as paper and pencils will help keep your family entertained during the displacement.

⬿ Don't forget your pets. Supplies should include:

- Pet food and water bowl
- Small bag of kitty litter
- Leash or harness
- Travel box and blanket
- Grooming brush, medication, and copies of your pet's medical records

⬿ If you are not able to take your pets when you evacuate, leave as much food, water, and kitty litter as possible in one area of the house. Be sure each pet has an ID tag. Post a note on the door indicating how many pets are in your house.

Disaster Kit for Vehicles

⬿ COMFORTS: coffee-can furnace (a candle nestled in sand will generate emergency heat), bottled water, set of plastic or paper plates, cups, and utensils, tissues, blankets, old jacket, and shoes or boots

⬿ EMERGENCY ASSISTANCE: booster cables, flares, fire extinguisher (the five-pound, A-B-C type), battery-powered radio, flashlight, lantern, extra batteries, matches, maps, paper towels, large plastic bags, first-aid kit and manual, and paper and pencil

    ✐ WINTER WEATHER: antifreeze, de-icing spray, windshield brush and scraper, sand or kitty litter for tire traction if you're stuck in the snow, and a small shovel

    ✐ TIRES: tire repair kit and a pump

    ✐ TOOLS: ax, hammer, screwdrivers, rope, and clean rags

What's the Final Step?

You've set up your necessary medical supplies and papers, made some changes to make your house safer, decided on an emergency plan, and started preparing a disaster kit. You're on a roll.

    How can you maintain a ready, alert status? Stay vigilant and incorporate health and safety into your daily routines. If you have a calm and orderly home, you can personally decrease many health risks and dangers to your family. Now it's time to *Set Up a Routine to Control Clutter and Chaos That You Might Encounter in an Emergency.*

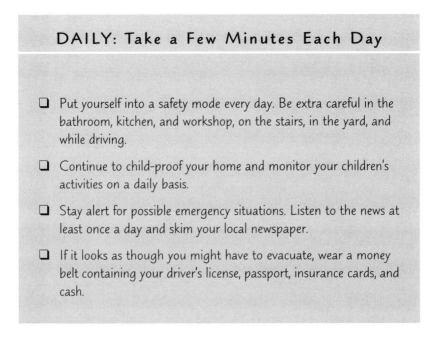

DAILY: Take a Few Minutes Each Day

❑ Put yourself into a safety mode every day. Be extra careful in the bathroom, kitchen, and workshop, on the stairs, in the yard, and while driving.

❑ Continue to child-proof your home and monitor your children's activities on a daily basis.

❑ Stay alert for possible emergency situations. Listen to the news at least once a day and skim your local newspaper.

❑ If it looks as though you might have to evacuate, wear a money belt containing your driver's license, passport, insurance cards, and cash.

WEEKLY: Take a Few Minutes Each Week

❑ Periodically make sure that medications are taken correctly by family members.

❑ Check for prescription medicines that need to be refilled.

❑ When you get a medication for the first time, add the information to your daily meds list and file the medication information sheet in your PERMANENT BUSINESS AND HOUSEHOLD health folder.

❑ While housecleaning, fix potential problems, such as a frayed cord or a child protection gate that doesn't lock securely.

MONTHLY or ANNUALLY: Take 30 Minutes

❑ Review emergency plans with your family twice a year.

❑ Check the disaster kit and replace water bottles and food that may have spoiled or gone stale every three months.

❑ Update the papers in the disaster kit every six months. Pull out and file old papers then add the latest information to the kit.

❑ Check smoke detectors and carbon monoxide detectors once a month. Change their batteries once a year.

Chapter 13

HOME OFFICE

∿∿∿∿∿∿∿∿∿∿∿∿∿∿∿∿

Help!

You'd really like to set up a full-time office at home or perhaps it's time to whip your home or work office into shape. Not only do the room, papers, and supplies need to be organized but you need to be more efficient. Digging through mounds of memos, losing documents, and missing deadlines won't help your business or your peace of mind. Can you do something about it? Rest assured. Here's the plan.

The First Part of the Plan Is *Schedule It*

Consult the calendar and set aside a few days to start fixing up a home office. For example:

- ✏ Wednesday after work might be a good time to shop for a new desk.
- ✏ Listen to a ball game or music while you arrange the furniture and set up all the supplies.

The Next Part of the Plan Is *Organize It*

The following six steps will help you control your clutter.

1st Step: Location, Location, Location
THE SETUP

Where can you set up for business in your home? The minimum requirements include space for a desk, phone, and lamp, room for the equipment necessary for your particular home business, shelving or filing cabinets, and sufficient office supplies. The right atmosphere for working and security for protecting all your documents would be additional priorities.

Space   It may be difficult to find a good spot for your work space in a smaller home, condominium, or apartment. If you live in a larger house, you may have lots of family members swirling around. Frequently people set up an office in the basement or convert a spare bedroom. My brother built a small barn just behind his full house and retreats to do all his work there. If necessary, get innovative and create an area in the dining room or clear a spot under the stairway:

- Use attractive file cabinets, screens, or a bookcase as a room divider.
- Provide space for a coworker or a secretary.
- Set up an off-limits schedule if you're working in an area that family members occasionally need to use.

Atmosphere   Think about what's important to your working environment. Choose a place where you can concentrate and not be distracted by movies, by someone else's music, or by the kids monkeying around:

- Sit with your back to the window if the view will be too distracting.
- Provide a room heater or a fan depending on the season.
- Add decorative touches for a more relaxing atmosphere.
- Plug in a radio or CD player.

Security   Don't allow children and pets to race through your office and possibly scatter organized papers:

⌗ Keep the door locked if there are important and sensitive materials involving financial, legal, medical, or personal details about clients or patients or if you're a secret agent.

⌗ Use a safe or lockbox if you keep a lot of cash on hand or if you deal with such items as diamonds, stocks and bonds, or federal documents.

2nd Step: Purchasing

SHOPPING LIST

Decide what furniture, equipment, and supplies are needed. If money is not a problem, choose high-quality items that will last. If you are working within a budget, watch for sales at office supply stores or buy inexpensive desks, tables, and storage shelves at home-goods stores or thrift shops.

Furniture

⌗ Desk

⌗ Computer table

⌗ Card table

⌗ Long table for office equipment and work space

⌗ Comfortable chair and footstool

⌗ Two-drawer file cabinets that are easier to move around; stack them for a four-door look

⌗ Plastic storage bins on wheels for papers or supplies

⌗ Book and storage shelves

⌗ Four desktop stackable trays

⌗ Two desktop folder stands

⌗ Plastic tray with slots for paper

⌗ Desktop or floor lamp

⌗ Shredder

⌗ Small safe or lockbox, if necessary

⌗ Wastebasket

Tips for additional work space:

- Instead of a long table, buy a board and lay it on top of several two-drawer file cabinets to create a counter
- Place a card table or two-drawer file cabinet next to your desk for additional work space

Plug It In

- Telephone
- Answering machine
- Computer, printer, scanner
- Fax machine
- Personal digital assistants (PDAs)
- Home copy machine
- Clock
- Electric pencil sharpener
- Calculator

Additional tips:

- Be sure that you have enough electrical outlets and telephone jacks.
- Tie equipment cords together with twist ties and move the cords out of sight as much as possible.

Electronic Supplies

- Computer diskettes
- Computer paper
- Blank CD/DVD media
- Media organizing boxes
- Fax paper
- Fax printer rolls or cartridges
- Ink or toner cartridges
- Batteries

Office Equipment

- Bulletin board
- Business card holder
- Cash box
- Hole punch
- Hot glue gun
- Letter opener
- Magnifying glass
- Paper cutter
- Phone card holder
- Stapler and staple remover

The Supply Depot

- Binder clips, all sizes
- Correction fluid
- Drawer organizing trays
- Erasers
- Glue sticks
- Paper clips, regular and small
- Pens, pencils, felt-tip pens
- Rubber bands
- Ruler and yardstick
- Scissors
- Stamps and stamp pad
- Staples
- Tape dispenser
- Transparent tape

Correspondence Supplies

- Address labels
- Business envelopes
- Greeting card assortment
- Mailers

- Manila envelopes
- Office stationery and envelopes
- Personal stationery
- Postage stamps
- Shipping supplies, including labels, pouches, packs, tubes, and boxes

Paper Products

- Binder notebooks
- Clipboards
- Day planner
- Desktop calendar
- File folder dividers
- File folder labels
- File folders
- Folders with two pockets
- Hanging file folders
- Index cards, assorted sizes
- Labels, assorted sizes and colors
- Laminating sheets or rolls
- Legal pads and notepads
- Lined paper
- Plastic protector sheets
- Sticky notes

3rd Step: Setting Up the Office

IN PLACE

Whether fixing up an existing home or work office or setting up a new one, it's probably a pretty disorganized mess. Work your way around the room and track down all those clutter culprits.

Cleanup Crew   Sort through every area of the office and discard all obsolete, outdated, and useless memos, books, magazines, catalogs, business papers, and receipts:

- Rip out personal and financial information and drop them in your shredding box.

- Toss out broken equipment and empty supply containers.

- Remove everything that doesn't belong in an office, such as a bag of old clothes, stacks of newspapers, and boxes of household odds and ends.

- If necessary, get out the broom, mop, vacuum cleaner, or dust rag and spruce things up.

The Desk Setup   Look at the file cabinets, book and storage shelves, and long table and decide on the most efficient place for your desk:

- If you don't have a computer desk, set the computer, printer, and media storage box on the desk.

- Angle a card table or a two-drawer file cabinet nearby to add desktop space.

- Set a desktop calendar or day planner, a phone card holder, and a business card holder by the phone.

- Keep a few phone books in a drawer along with a phone list in a plastic folder of your most frequently called contacts and their business numbers.

- If pens and paper keep mysteriously disappearing, tape a small notepad by the phone and tie the pen with a string or buy a pen on a chain.

- Set out a tape dispenser, stapler, and box of tissues.

- Fill some drawer organizing trays with the usual pens, paper clips, sticky notes, glue stick, and scissors.

- Tuck a calculator and notepads in a drawer.

- It's handy to have a folder at the desk with menus from your favorite local restaurants.

Long Table   Set up a long table flush against the wall for office equipment and extra work space:

- Line up the fax and home copy machines and an electric pencil sharpener. Add the paper cutter, hole punch, and plastic tray with an assortment of stationery, lined paper, and computer paper.

- Use a box or tray to hold all your PDAs.
- Plug in the shredder by the table. Set up a box or the lid from a computer box in which to stack papers until you're ready for a little shredding party.

The Supply Stockpile Clear and dust all the storage shelves and then decide how to organize them:

- Gather small boxes to help store items. For example, put bottles of correction fluid in a small box and then use the lid to hold paper clips.
- Store office supplies together, including separate boxes or plastic trays with separators for pencils, pens, rubber bands, staples, and the usual desk supplies.
- Store equipment supplies together, including batteries, blank diskettes, fax supplies, and ink cartridges.
- Store paper supplies together, including computer paper, file folders, labels, lined paper, and stationery.

Bookshelves Bookshelves are as necessary to your office setup as a desk. Whether they are wall-mounted or freestanding, use them to help you organize:

- The following items can be stored on bookshelves:
  - Company handouts and booklets
  - Sets of promotional packets
  - Books—reference
  - Books—business-related
  - Business newsletters—back issues
  - Phone books—extra ones that cover your service area
  - Professional magazines—back issues
- Set up a TO READ shelf for items that maybe someday you'll get around to reading:
  - Place articles, pamphlets, and newsletters in one spot.
  - Put current issues of magazines in another.

• Stack catalogs that you'd like to browse through when you have some time.

File Cabinet   File cabinets can hold more than files. Consider storing the following items there:

✐ Business-related catalogs

✐ Company guidelines, handbooks, manuals, and policies

✐ Instruction manuals for all your home office equipment

PERMANENT BUSINESS FOLDERS

Look at ways to make your files more efficient:

✐ Check each folder and dump as much outdated material as possible.

✐ File the folders in categories so all the client folders will be in one section and all the invoices will be in another section.

✐ File the following materials together. Skip any subjects that don't apply to your business and add your own subjects as needed:

• ACCOUNTING, including folders for ledgers and receipt books
• CLIENTS, including a folder for each client, company, patient, student, or specific projects
• COMPANY INFORMATION, including folders for board member profiles and company history
• CONFERENCES, including folders with schedules, notes, and handouts that you'd like to save
• FINANCIAL, including folders for past petty cash receipts and bank information
• FORMS, including folders for permission slips and reimbursement forms
• INSURANCE, including a folder for each company along with coverage information
• INVENTORY, including folders for equipment and supplies
• MARKETING, including folders for pamphlets and press releases
• PERSONNEL, including folders for hiring guidelines and personnel records
• PROJECTS, including a separate folder for each project

- PURCHASING, including folders for purchasing guidelines and purchase orders
- STATISTICS, including folders for circulation statistics
- TAXES, including folders for tax forms specific to your business and tax statements

BUSINESS WITH STYLE

Now that your home office is looking efficient and organized, why not give it a touch of class with a few decorative ideas?

- Place some plants, real or artificial, on the desk, long table, bookshelf, or file cabinet.
- Hang a few attractive and tasteful landscape paintings, scenic photos, antique maps, or diplomas and certificates.
- Angle the desk across a corner.
- Provide a comfy chair for visitors.
- Add a floor or ceiling fan.
- Buy solid-color window curtains or consider blinds or shades.
- Set up a small coffee maker for coffee and tea. Store an assortment of coffee and tea, creamer and sugar, and cups, saucers, spoons, and napkins.
- Add a small refrigerator or water cooler.

4th Step: Calendars, Trays, Folders, Envelopes, and Incoming Papers

WHAT DO I DO WITH ALL THIS?

Well now, it's looking like a real office and you can actually see the top of your desk. How often does that happen? Unfortunately, you know it won't last for long. Your desk soon will be completely covered with papers. We definitely need a plan here. Let's set up some calendars, trays, folders, and envelopes to help keep track of everything.

Calendar Girl or Boy   We can't conduct business without our calendar or day planner:

- Be sure that all appointments and deadlines are jotted down on the calendar.

⊘ Keep the calendar or day planner on your desk and always put it in the same compartment when using your briefcase or tote bag.

TO DO: YEARLY List   A great deal of business is routine. Reports frequently are due monthly, quarterly, or annually. Newsletters, requests for grants—most of the time we know the exact deadlines, so how come we continue to be surprised and unprepared?

⊘ Set up a permanent TO DO: YEARLY list that includes all the routine projects and general deadlines for each month.

⊘ Keep the list with your desktop calendar and check it every week. For example:
January
    1ST WEEK: Holiday thank-you notes to clients
    2ND WEEK: Monday—board meeting
        Prepare for annual presentation third week of February
    3RD WEEK: Client newsletter mailing
    4TH WEEK: Monthly director's report due

PARKING PAPERS

With so much paper continually coming in, it's necessary to prioritize and decide what has to be handled immediately, within the week, or at a future date. If all your documents are stored in a logical manner then you won't lose or forget them. Set up places to park these pesky papers in trays, folders, or envelopes until you're ready to actually deal with them.

Stackable Trays   Set up a first-line system to control the flow of paper in and out of your office:

⊘ Start by labeling four stackable trays:
1. MAIL—IN, including all current mail and messages.
2. MAIL—OUT, including items to be mailed and notes or memos to coworkers.
3. SECRETARY, or use just your secretary's first name, including an instruction note asking for a hundred copies by noon on Thursday.
4. TO BE FILED, the most hated tray of all. The good thing is

that even though it's stacked to the ceiling, this is finished business that just needs to be filed away.

✐ Place the first three trays on your desk, card table, or two-drawer file cabinet.

✐ Set the TO BE FILED tray a little further away, possibly on top of a bank of file cabinets.

TO DO: DAILY Folders   You can't run a successful business without these folders:

✐ Label four index cards:
   1. TO DO: TODAY—ASAP
   2. TO DO: MESSAGES
   3. TO DO: THIS WEEK
   4. TO DO: IDEAS—FUTURE PROJECTS

✐ Set up two folders, the kind with two inside pockets, that are the same color, such as red:

   • Open up one folder and tape index card number 1 to the left pocket and index card number 2 to the right pocket. Place a stiff divider sheet in the MESSAGES pocket. At the top of the sheet write PRIORITY MESSAGES IN FRONT.
   • Tape index cards number 3 and 4 to the inside pockets of the other red folder.

✐ Place both of the folders open and near your stackable trays and immediately file all incoming papers.

TO BE PAID and PETTY CASH RECEIPTS Folders   Set up a system to keep track of daily bills and receipts:

✐ Write TO BE PAID and the name of each month on twelve file folders. For example: TO BE PAID—JULY.

✐ Write PETTY CASH RECEIPTS and the name of each month on a separate business envelope and place them in a folder.

✐ Store the twelve TO BE PAID folders and the PETTY CASH RECEIPTS folder in a handy desk drawer.

✐ Keep the folders in order by month, always placing the current month in front.

5th Step: Priority Folders

IN EASY REACH

Yes, there are more clutter culprits to organize. Ain't it awful? No wonder it's so hard to keep on top of all those papers. Let's try to trim it down a little and set up some folders for DAILY BUSINESS and SPECIAL PROJECTS.

DAILY BUSINESS Folders   These folders are for routine, ongoing responsibilities and commitments. So you won't lose track of important information, each week put the necessary papers into the DAILY BUSINESS folders and keep them in a desktop folder stand. When it's time to start getting ready for a meeting or to handle a problem, all the pertinent information will be in a specific folder rather than buried under piles or scattered around the room:

- Use only one color, such as yellow, for all the DAILY BUSINESS folders. Stick a large identifying label at the top of each folder and place them in a desktop folder stand within easy reach.

- When that item of business is complete, file all the final copies of reports and meetings in the permanent file cabinet. Leave the DAILY BUSINESS folders on your desk and continue to use them for storing the latest memo about an upcoming meeting or a new personnel concern.

- DAILY BUSINESS *folders* might include:
  - COMPANY REPS
  - KEY CLIENTS
  - MAINTENANCE AND REPAIRS
  - MEETINGS: BOARD
  - MEETINGS: DEPARTMENT
  - PERSONNEL: CONCERNS AND PROBLEMS
  - PERSONNEL: SCHEDULING
  - PURCHASING

SPECIAL PROJECTS Folders   Special activities and projects keep cropping up. You don't want to mix these papers in with your normal daily business. The following folders are for temporary or one-time clients and for special committees, events, or reports:

✐ Use only one color, such as blue, for all SPECIAL PROJECTS folders. Use an identifying label on each one and place them in a separate desktop folder stand.

✐ Keep all important papers in the specific folder for whichever project you're working on. When it's over, store necessary items in the permanent file cabinet and dump everything else.

✐ Put a new blank label over the old label and place the folder at the back of your folders. You know there will always be an unexpected project popping up. Now you'll be ready for it.

✐ SPECIAL PROJECTS *folders* might include:
  • CONFERENCE SPEECH
  • FUNDRAISER
  • LAWSUIT
  • NEW EQUIPMENT PURCHASING DECISION
  • RESEARCH FOR A CLIENT
  • SOCIAL EVENTS

SPECIAL PROJECTS and DAILY BUSINESS folders are used frequently. If there's no more room on your desk, put these two desktop folder stands on top of the nearby two-drawer file cabinet or on the long table.

If you prefer, keep these folders handy inside your desk drawer. Place the DAILY BUSINESS folders in the front of the drawer and all the SPECIAL PROJECTS folders behind them.

THE TICKLER FILE

The TICKLER file offers a different approach for organizing your papers and involves an accordion-style file. Check Chapter 14 to see if this is a system that you might like to try.

6th Step: The Daily Work Routine

WHAT'S YOUR PRIORITY?

I've just spent a lot of time discussing how to keep track of incoming papers associated with a ton of projects. Let's put all the advice together to create a daily work routine. Our goal is to eliminate piles of miscellaneous materials so that you can function more efficiently. Every note, letter, message, invoice, and scrap of paper should go straight into a tray, folder, or envelope. Don't forget, you do own a wastebasket—lots of papers belong in there.

Check Messages   It's important to set aside time each morning to check messages and to work on the priorities for the day. However, in spite of our best intentions, it's not always that easy. You walk into your home office and within twenty minutes or less you can totally lose it. When you are so overwhelmed by all those things you need to address what can you do about it? Let's take it a step at a time and see if we can't make some order out of chaos. For example:

- The boss called and needs information: write a reminder note and put it in the TO DO: TODAY—ASAP folder.
- The fax clicks on and suddenly jams up: fix it immediately.
- A client calls to set up a meeting for next week and will need you to bring a specific form: add the time and place of the meeting to your desk calendar and a reminder to bring the form.
- Get back to work on that request from your boss: check the note in your folder, find the info, and e-mail it to your boss.
- Check previous notes in the MESSAGES folder and new phone, e-mail, and fax messages: delete all the junk stuff, choose only priority messages, and either answer them immediately or jot down the name, number, and request and pop the notes into one of your TO DO folders. For example:
  - A colleague e-mails a fact sheet about a project that will begin in several months: print a copy, attach a note, and drop it in the TO DO: IDEAS—FUTURE PROJECTS folder.
  - A supervisor sends a fax to suggest that you look into a project at another company: put it in the TO DO: THIS WEEK folder.
  - A friend left a call to suggest golf next weekend: put a note in front of the MESSAGES folder to call back right after lunch.
- Quickly check your less important messages: take notes and drop them in back of the MESSAGES folder or put the notes in the TO DO folders.

Mail Call   Don't let the mail pile up and turn into another big project. Sort it every day and slip the items into a folder or tray:

🖋 Junk mail: rip out personal and financial information, put it in the shredding box, and toss the rest.

🖋 Bills and invoices: put in the TO BE PAID folders for that month.

🖋 A receipt and copy of the latest tax ID statement: put in the TO BE FILED tray.

🖋 A request to speak at a local meeting: put in the TO DO: TODAY—ASAP folder.

🖋 A registration form for a conference you'd like to attend: put in the TO DO: THIS WEEK folder.

🖋 Professional magazines, newsletters, and catalogs: put on the TO READ shelf.

🖋 A receipt in your wallet for a recent purchase: put in the PETTY CASH RECEIPTS envelope for that month.

Priority Projects   What absolutely must be done today? Set your priorities. For example:

🖋 Petty cash receipts need to be totaled by next week: put last month's PETTY CASH RECEIPTS envelope in the tray for your SECRETARY.

🖋 Bills need to be paid: check the TO BE PAID folder, pull out the bills that you intend to pay, and start preparing the checks.

🖋 Work on a presentation for the upcoming meeting next week: pull out the DAILY BUSINESS folder for meetings and revise your speech on the computer.

🖋 There's a new project that you need to get going on: pull out the SPECIAL PROJECTS folder, turn on the computer, and use the checklist and notes to outline the project.

AT THE END OF EACH DAY

Never just get up and walk out of your office. Plan on a few minutes to tidy up. Yes, in spite of our great system, sometimes things happen so fast we still end up with clutter culprits. Quickly straighten up the room and sort miscellaneous papers so you don't have to start the next day with a big old batch of litter on your desk:

🖋 Keep a clean and classy office. Toss papers, candy wrappers, and coffee cups into the trash and dump it regularly.

✐ Take a few minutes to sort leftover papers and pop them into the correct tray, folder, or envelope.

✐ What are the priorities for the next day? Quickly look through the calendar, trays, TO DO: DAILY folders, SPECIAL PROJECTS folders, TO BE PAID folders, or the TICKLER file. Pull out the bills to be paid and the papers and folders that you will need to work on tomorrow. Stack them neatly and in priority order.

What's the Final Step?

Your office looks great and is running smoothly—for the time being. How can you maintain this level of efficiency? Now it's time to *Set Up a Routine to Control Clutter and Chaos*.

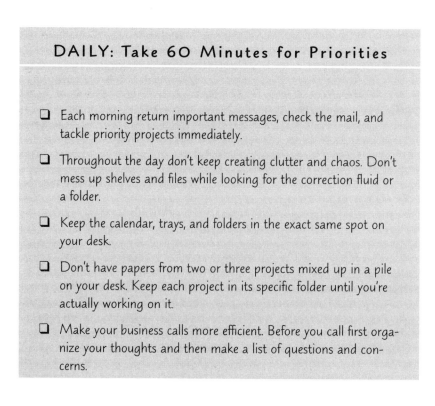

DAILY: Take 60 Minutes for Priorities

❑ Each morning return important messages, check the mail, and tackle priority projects immediately.

❑ Throughout the day don't keep creating clutter and chaos. Don't mess up shelves and files while looking for the correction fluid or a folder.

❑ Keep the calendar, trays, and folders in the exact same spot on your desk.

❑ Don't have papers from two or three projects mixed up in a pile on your desk. Keep each project in its specific folder until you're actually working on it.

❑ Make your business calls more efficient. Before you call first organize your thoughts and then make a list of questions and concerns.

❑ Before you leave for the day, quickly straighten up the office and set up the priorities for the next day.

WEEKLY: Take 60 Minutes

❑ Regularly deposit cash and checks at the bank.

❑ Each Friday take ten minutes to check your business calendar and TO DO: YEARLY list to note any upcoming deadlines.

❑ Clean out and organize your briefcase or tote bag.

❑ Before attending a business meeting or function, triple-check that you've packed your speech, handouts, tickets, and other vital items.

❑ Turn on some music, grab papers in your TO BE FILED tray, and file as many as you can in fifteen or twenty minutes.

❑ After the weekly housecleaning take another twenty minutes in your home office to quickly dust, vacuum, and straighten.

❑ After cleaning, check the shelves and make a shopping list of needed office equipment and paper supplies.

MONTHLY or ANNUALLY: Take Several Afternoons

❑ Give your whole office a good cleaning twice a year. Wash windows and the carpet, sort and rearrange the shelves, or move the furniture around for a more efficient and attractive layout.

❑ Once a year toss or shred anything that's obsolete or has been replaced by more current information.

❑ Reorganize your folders, if necessary. Add new folders, change the names of some, or store them in a different section of the file cabinet.

❑ Regularly check to see if your computer and PDA files need to be updated, deleted, or reorganized.

Chapter 14

PAPERWORK — DAILY

Help!

Those clutter culprits just keep coming at you. Every day you empty your pockets of receipts, you bring home papers from work or school, and you get tons of mail courtesy of the good old U.S. Post Office. Can you do something about it? Yes! Here's the plan.

The First Part of the Plan Is *Schedule It*

Organizing your mail and paperwork is one of the most difficult systems to maintain. You're on top of it today, but you know that tomorrow there'll be another load of bills and business papers staring you in the face. One thing that can help you is a sorting system. Make the time to set it up. For example:

- Zero in on a spare afternoon or evening. Label folders and envelopes in which to file bills to be paid, receipts, personal letters to be answered, and new photos.

✐ On another day watch a movie while you do a little paper catch-up, such as adding new addresses or e-mails to your address book and clipping coupons.

The Next Part of the Plan Is *Organize It*

The following three steps will help you control your clutter.

1st Step: Mail and Paperwork

SET UP A SYSTEM

A few easy changes can help you avoid paper pileups:

✐ Choose a spot where your daily mail can sit until you're ready to open it. Check Chapter 13 for details about setting up a home office.

✐ Since you're probably not going to write checks and handle business decisions each day, you'll need a place to put bills and letters until you're ready to deal with them.

✐ Set up folders and envelopes for organizing your bills and business papers. You can put them in a drawer or place them in stand-up or stackable trays.

✐ Label three folders (use folders with two pockets):
  • TO DO—TO BE PAID: bills, tickets to order, catalog orders
  • TO DO—BUSINESS AND HOUSEHOLD: personal letters, decisions to make about insurance, a bid from one of the two roofers you've contacted
  • TO DO—TO BE FILED: papers to be filed in permanent folders

✐ Label four business envelopes:
  • CATCHALL: coupons, lottery tickets, sales information
  • PHOTOS: individual photos and store photo packages
  • RECEIPTS: all receipts from the bank and from new purchases
  • TO SHRED: just the ripped-out parts with personal information

✐ Set up a spot for magazines, newspapers, and catalogs.

2nd Step: Daily Habit

DO IT DAILY

Put yourself on autopilot and handle your mail each day:

- ✐ Sort mail into folders and envelopes every day.
- ✐ Place photos and receipts into envelopes.
- ✐ Dump as much junk mail as you can in the trash or in your recycling bin.

THE TICKLER FILE

If you're not comfortable with the folder and envelope system, try out the TICKLER file, aptly named because your fingers tickle through the days of the month. Here's how to set it up:

- ✐ Buy two expanding file folders with built-in dividers for the days of the month or make two sets of folders for each day of the month.
- ✐ As you sort mail, file all bills to be paid, invoices, papers, birthday cards to send, tickets, directions to a business meeting, and reminder notes for follow-up calls behind the days that you plan to deal with them.
- ✐ File all the papers for next month into the second TICKLER file.
- ✐ Every day check the current date to see what needs to be done.
- ✐ At the beginning of the new month, switch to the second TICKLER file. The first file should be empty and ready to be filled up with papers for the following month.

3rd Step: Weekly Habit

DO IT WEEKLY

Take a little time each week to whittle down some of the paperwork piles:

- ✐ Pull out bills from the TO DO—TO BE PAID folder:
  - • Pay bills on the Internet or write the checks and prepare them for mailing.
  - • Balance your check register.

- Place paid statements and receipts in the TO DO—TO BE FILED folder.

✐ Check the TO DO—BUSINESS AND HOUSEHOLD folder:

- Handle paperwork and make your business decisions.
- Respond to invitations and send thank-you notes and birthday and sympathy cards.
- Place all papers to keep in the TO DO—TO BE FILED folder.

✐ Check the RECEIPTS envelope:

- Toss receipts for smaller, everyday expenditures.
- Save receipts for credit and debit card purchases until they are paid off.
- Save receipts for items that you might return.
- Place receipts for expensive purchases in the TO DO—TO BE FILED folder.

✐ Paper catch-up:

- Add new phone numbers and e-mail addresses to your address book.
- Toss out expired coupons and sales notices.
- Clip magazine and newspaper articles to save.

✐ Filing festival:

- Place articles and pamphlets in GENERAL INFORMATION, ACTION, and PERSONAL INTEREST folders, which will be discussed in Chapter 16.
- Take papers from the TO DO—TO BE FILED folder and place them in your file cabinet in their permanent folders. Chapter 16 also will provide a list of subjects to help you organize the permanent folders in your file cabinet.

What's the Final Step?

Through rain, sleet, or snow, the mail's going to be delivered to your door. You have a choice to let it pile up and become a monster mess or to get into the above daily and weekly habits. These habits will help you take charge and eliminate a lot of frustration and hassle. No more clutter culprits or late fees or missing important deadlines—lots more peace of mind.

Now it's time to *Set Up a Routine to Control Clutter and Chaos*.

DAILY: Take 5 to 10 Minutes

- ❑ Keep all TO DO folders and envelopes in the same place.
- ❑ Catch your favorite talk show or game show while sorting your mail, receipts, and photos.
- ❑ Don't let mail get scattered about.
- ❑ Automatically place all items that require action in the TO DO folders and envelopes. Toss the rest.

WEEKLY: Take 1 to 2 Hours

- ❑ Once a week pay bills and handle your paperwork.
- ❑ Consider paying all the bills on one day and working on the papers in the TO DO—BUSINESS AND HOUSEHOLD folder on another day.
- ❑ If you're really busy, put a casserole or roast in the oven (don't forget to set the timer), do some paperwork, and then enjoy dinner.

Chapter 15

PAPERWORK — BACKLOG

Help!

OK. You've totally lost it. Your paper pileup is no longer a couple of months' worth. It's been building up for several years and could now be considered a fire hazard. You have a perfect case of uncontrollable clutter. Can you do something about it? Yes! Let's dig in. Here's the plan.

The First Part of the Plan Is *Schedule It*

Check your calendar to see if this is the week that you might actually deal with your backlog of papers. If you have boxes and boxes of papers to sort, you can stretch out the project over several weeks. For example:

✐ Every evening sort a few stacks of papers while you're watching the news or your favorite prime-time TV shows.

The Next Part of the Plan Is *Organize It*

The following three steps will help you control your clutter.

1st Step: Sorting Station

SET UP A SYSTEM

It's a monumental mess. How do you get started sorting through your paper backlog? Don't worry. Just take it one step at a time:

- Stack all your papers together in some boxes.
- Choose a spot, such as the couch, dining room table, or floor, where you can leave piles of papers for a while. Pick a place where kids, cats, and dogs can't race through and undo all your work.
- Label three trash bags:
  - DUMP IT
  - RECYCLE IT
  - SHRED IT
- Label four boxes or plastic baskets:
  - TO BE PAID
  - BUSINESS AND HOUSEHOLD
  - TO BE FILED
  - PHOTOS

2nd Step: The Big Decision

KEEPERS

Before you start sifting through the papers, how can you decide what you really need to keep?

- How long should you keep important papers? Use the following categories:
  - KEEP FOREVER, includes birth certificates, marriage or divorce papers, military service records, and Social Security cards
  - KEEP UPDATED COPIES, includes home, car, and life insurance policies, loan agreements, wills, and pay stubs
  - KEEP FOR SEVEN YEARS, includes bank statements and income tax returns

- KEEP FOR ONLY THE CURRENT YEAR, includes credit card and utility statements
- KEEP UNTIL SOLD OR NO LONGER OWNED, includes investment certificates, receipts for appliances and furniture, service contracts, and vehicle titles

MOVE 'EM ON OUT

You'll never miss all that outdated paperwork. Get rid of as much as you can.

To Dump

- Toss out or recycle anything that's outdated (especially all those catalogs you so diligently saved).
- Toss out or recycle anything that you have a second copy of—you (usually) only need one.
- Throw junk mail into the trash or into your recycling bin.

To Shred or Not to Shred

- Don't shred whole pages. Just rip out the small sections with your name, address, and personal information.
- Shred documents that list your name, address, phone number, Social Security number, financial and medical information, and anything you don't want to share with the world.

ESTIMATED TIME

So how long will this take? Who knows. Oh, oh. Did I say that out loud? Well, the thing is, the longer that you've gone without sorting and filing, the longer it will take you to work your way through your clutter culprits.

Remember: You have an option for making this a more pleasant project:

- Sort while you watch an afternoon talk show or an old movie.
- Sort while you listen to some new CDs or a book on tape.

3rd Step: Dig In

READY! SET! GO!

Lay out your three trash bags and four sorting boxes or baskets. Sit down, get comfy, and get started:

✐ Grab a piece of paper and toss it into the appropriate bag or box. For example:
- Last year's phone bill—SHRED IT
- This month's phone bill—TO BE PAID
- Picture of your son's brand-new baby (born two years ago)—PHOTOS
- Daughter's report card—TO BE FILED
- Blood test results from the doctor—TO BE FILED
- Registration form for a class—BUSINESS AND HOUSEHOLD
- Current pizza coupon—TO BE FILED
- Travel resort brochures that are several years old—DUMP IT or RECYCLE IT

✐ Keep working your way through the papers. Try to dump, recycle, and shred as much as you can.

What's the Final Step?

You've gotten rid of lots of papers and the rest are all sorted and just sitting in your four sorting boxes. What the heck do you do with them? Now it's time to *Set Up a Routine to Control Clutter and Chaos*.

WEEKLY: Take 1 to 2 Hours

❑ Get out the TO DO folders and envelopes you use for sorting the daily mail. Take all the papers out of the following three sorting boxes and place them in their respective TO DO folders:

- TO BE PAID papers go into the TO DO—TO BE PAID folder.
- BUSINESS AND HOUSEHOLD papers go into the TO DO—BUSINESS AND HOUSEHOLD folder.
- PHOTOS go into the TO DO—PHOTOS envelope.

❑ These papers have been buried in piles too long. Don't let them sit for another month in your TO DO folders. Handle these priority items as soon as possible.

There's just one box left. The big one—the TO BE FILED sorting box. Now what are you supposed to do with this mind-boggling batch of papers? Let's move ahead to Chapter 16. It can help you decide the best place to file your papers so that you can easily find them again.

Chapter 16

PAPERWORK — FILING FESTIVAL

Help!

You've just sorted through boxes of old papers and discovered paid receipts, investment statements, medical exam information, travel brochures, personal letters, and pay stubs. Your TO BE FILED sorting box is stuffed with a little under a ton of clutter culprits. Now what? Can you do something about it? Sure thing! Here's the plan.

The First Part of the Plan Is *Schedule It*

In Chapter 15 you put a lot of materials into your TO DO folders and dumped a lot of stuff. Now it's time to dig into the TO BE FILED box of papers and sort them into special categories. For example:

✐ On Tuesday after dinner, label folders for GENERAL INFOR-MATION and ACTION. They'll help you organize the regular papers that keep dropping in on you.

✐ On Thursday start getting your PERMANENT BUSINESS AND HOUSEHOLD folders and PERSONAL INTEREST folders in order.

✐ After you've labeled your folders, take a half hour each day while listening to the news to sort papers and pop them into the correct folders.

The Next Part of the Plan Is *Organize It*

The following three steps will help you control your clutter.

1st Step: GENERAL INFORMATION Folders and ACTION Folders

GENERAL INFORMATION FOLDERS
What are you supposed to do with all those papers in your TO BE FILED box? Place them in four different categories: GENERAL IN-FORMATION, ACTION, PERMANENT BUSINESS AND HOUSE-HOLD, and PERSONAL INTEREST.

Let's start with the GENERAL INFORMATION folders:

✐ Create a reference section with several GENERAL INFORMA-TION folders filed next to your phone books. Set up as many as you need.

✐ Don't lose track of important information. Each week put materials into one of the GENERAL INFORMATION folders.

✐ GENERAL INFORMATION folders might include:
  • CLUB AND GROUP MEMBERSHIPS, including golf club, chorus, church group, car club, theater group, and bowling league
  • DIRECTIONS, including computer map printouts, directions drawn on a napkin by your friend, and auto club maps
  • ENTERTAINMENT, including information about fun things to do in the area, restaurant reviews, upcoming musical events, art

fairs, home tours, museums, ball game schedules, and lists of parks, tennis clubs, swimming pools, and fishing and camping grounds
- SCHOOL, including phone numbers, list of your children's teachers and classes, school calendar, lunch menu, school code of conduct, newsletters, and notes from teachers
- TAXES, including tax booklets, forms, and notes

ACTION FOLDERS

Instead of leaving papers in mixed-up piles, drop them into one of your ACTION folders:

✐ ACTION folders might include:
- ELECTION INFORMATION, including articles and pamphlets about current issues and candidates
- HOUSEHOLD PROJECTS, including estimates for repairs or renovations, measurements, and receipts
- LEGAL CONCERNS, including all paperwork for a current problem
- MEDICAL CONCERNS, including all paperwork for a current problem
- SPECIAL EVENTS, including wedding, graduation, or retirement party plans
- VACATION PLANS, including tickets, confirmation notices, articles, and pamphlets

✐ ACTION folders should be stacked together in your office area.

What follows is an example of how an ACTION folder might work for you. A family member is going through a health crisis, including a hospital stay. You've got enough to worry about without having to search for important medical papers, prescriptions, and hospital information. It's time to take action:

✐ Be kind to yourself and keep all this new medical information together in one folder.

After the patient has recovered, file any important papers in your permanent medical folders, toss unimportant papers, and put the empty folder with your office supplies.

2nd Step: PERMANENT BUSINESS AND HOUSEHOLD Folders

FINAL DESTINATION

File your most important papers in permanent folders. Then you can find your muffler warranty, tax information, investment papers, and mortgage documents whenever you need them:

- Buy inexpensive file cabinets or plastic drawers. You can even use regular cardboard boxes to store your papers.

- Buy several packets of file folders.

- If you file everything in straight alphabetical order, your insurance papers will be right between gardening tips and karate articles and your education records will be filed between decorating articles and exercise tips.

- Therefore, it's more useful to set up different sections so that PERMANENT BUSINESS AND HOUSEHOLD folders are in one section and PERSONAL INTEREST folders are filed together. Check out the itemized lists below of topics that you might like to use.

- Label the file cabinets or boxes so that you don't have to guess at the contents.

- Be sure that your spouse or legal representative knows how your papers are organized in case of an emergency.

- Consider storing really important papers in a fireproof box or in a bank safe-deposit box and keeping a photocopy of them in your office for quick reference.

- At least once a month, take the papers out of your TO DO—TO BE FILED folder and file them into your permanent folders.

PERMANENT BUSINESS AND HOUSEHOLD FOLDERS

Use this list to give you some ideas about what folders might be useful. Skip any subjects that don't apply to you and add your own subjects as needed.

Business/Financial

- Bank information and safe-deposit box key
- Bank statements
- Box of bank checks
- Contributions
- Credit union
- Income taxes
- Investments
- Pay stubs

Household/Family Records

- Documents, including birth certificate, marriage certificate, divorce papers, Social Security card, adoption papers, military papers, medals, naturalization papers, death certificate, and will:
  - Keep in one folder or in a safe-deposit box.
  - If you prefer, set up a separate folder for each.
- Education records
- Employment records
- Family (a folder for each family member, if necessary):
  - Include birth certificates, Social Security cards, birth announcements, baptism records, report cards, graduation program, wedding program, letters
- Friends:
  - Include mementos, letters, and articles about friends
- Household inventory
- Household maintenance and repair information:
  - Include name and brand of paint used in each room and information about major repairs and redecorating
  - Appliance and equipment instruction manuals
- Household receipts:
  - Include receipts for purchases, service contracts, and warranties
- Insurance:
  - Dental

- Health
- Homeowner
- Life
- Long-term care
- Vehicles
- Vision

- Journals and diaries

- Jury duty

- Keys (be sure to label each key)

- Legal information and records

- Medical information and records

- Monthly receipts for the last year:
  - Keep twelve business envelopes, one for each month.
  - Put all the January receipts for credit cards, utilities, and rent in the January envelope, the February receipts in the February envelope, and so on throughout the year.

- Mortgage and rent information and receipts

- Pets' health records and information

- Photo negatives

- Retirement records

- Security or alarm system information

- Subscription information

- Travel documents and official travel information

- Vehicle ownership and repair information

- Voting precinct information

3rd Step: PERSONAL INTEREST Folders

FINAL DESTINATION

Do you like to save lots of articles about all kinds of subjects? They aren't much help if you can't put your hands on them when you want them:

- Set up a separate drawer or box for your personal interest information.

⊘ Include articles, tips, and pamphlets about subjects that caught your attention.

⊘ Save certificates, awards, and mementos from groups and clubs that you belong to.

⊘ At least once a month, take the papers out of your TO DO—TO BE FILED folder and file them into your PERSONAL INTEREST folders.

PERSONAL INTEREST FOLDERS

Use this list to give yourself some ideas about what folders might be useful. Skip any subjects that don't apply to you and add your own subjects as needed:

⊘ Antiques

⊘ Art

⊘ Articles—Other (for articles you enjoyed and would like to save but that don't belong in any of the folders you have created)

⊘ Building and carpentry

⊘ Cartoons and humor

⊘ Child raising

⊘ Clothing and cosmetics

⊘ Clubs, groups, and organizations (a folder for each membership)

⊘ Computers

⊘ Cooking

⊘ Crafts

⊘ Decorating

⊘ Education articles

⊘ Exercise tips

⊘ Financial, budget, and investment articles

⊘ Gardening

⊘ Genealogy

⊘ Health, medicine, nutrition, and dieting articles

⊘ Hobbies (a folder for each)

⊘ Holiday ideas (a folder for each)

- Home improvement articles
- Hunting and fishing
- Internet articles
- Literature (book lists and reviews)
- Maintenance and repair tips and articles
- Maps
- Movies, theater, television
- Music
- Pet articles
- Relationship articles about dating and marriage tips
- Religion and church articles
- Self-help and psychology
- Sports
- Travel and vacation articles
- Travel and vacation mementos, including such things as brochures and large picture postcards

What's the Final Step?

You've got beautiful folders all ready and waiting. Let's figure out a system to keep those pesky papers from turning into problem piles. Now it's time to *Set Up a Routine to Control Clutter and Chaos*.

DAILY: Take 5 to 10 Minutes

❑ Store your TO DO folders in the same place. Keep all your papers inside those folders, not in piles or as clutter culprits scattered around the room.

❑ Don't let the mail get out of control. Do a quick sort each day and pop items into your TO DO folders.

WEEKLY: Take 5 to 20 Minutes

❑ Throughout the week squeeze in a few mini filing festivals: watch TV as you file papers into your GENERAL INFORMATION and ACTION folders; start the washing machine and then place important papers in your file cabinets; order a pizza and spend twenty minutes filing until it arrives; then relax and enjoy your reward.

Chapter 17

PARTIES AND OVERNIGHT GUESTS

Help!

You love to entertain but getting ready for parties and company leaves you totally frazzled. You need a plan so that you can actually enjoy your own parties. Can you do something about it? Party on! Here's the plan.

The First Part of the Plan Is *Schedule It*

This party is going to come off a lot more smoothly if you sit down and take a few minutes to set up your game plan. For example:

- Check your calendar and schedule in a shopping day for invitations and decorations.
- Pick an evening, park yourself in front of the TV, and write out invitations.

The Next Part of the Plan Is *Organize It*

The following five steps will help you control your clutter.

1st Step: You're Having a Party
ADVANCE PLANNING

Don't worry about trying to impress people. Remind yourself that you just want everyone to have a good time in your home. OK. What's the plan?

Theme   First you'll need to decide on the theme or purpose of your party:

- Is this an elegant Christmas gathering, a casual Super Bowl bash, or a circus birthday party for a five-year-old?

Invitations   Your next step is to prepare a guest list:

- Buy invitations and stamps.
- Address, stamp, and mail the invitations.

Refreshments   Choose the food, snacks, and beverages that you'd like to serve:

- Make a shopping list or make arrangements with a caterer.
- Are there any special requests or dietary concerns for certain guests?

Entertainment   Decide on the type of entertainment and activities that you'd like to offer your guests:

- Schedule musicians, a disc jockey, or clowns.
- Decide on background music or music for dancing.
- Select videos or DVDs, playing cards, and board games.
- Do you want to set up for playing pool or Ping-Pong in the basement, or badminton, croquet, and swimming in the backyard?

- Plan on lots of games and activities for a children's party.
- Decide on gifts, photo albums, or special photo displays.

Decorations   Does this party require decorating, or will you only need a few flower arrangements?

- Make a list of decorations, flowers, and party favors.
- Do you need to borrow or rent tables, chairs, a tent, or other items?

GET SOME HELP
You don't have to do it all yourself. Where do you need help?

- If necessary, make arrangements for the kids to stay with a babysitter.
- Arrange with family and friends to assist with cooking, grilling, serving drinks, setting up the music, and chaperoning the children.
- Consider hiring a bartender and waiters.
- Give yourself a break and hire someone to clean the house before the party.

SET YOUR PRIORITIES AND DEADLINES
After you decide on the details for the party, figure out your plan for actually getting everything done:

- Look at the calendar and jot down the things that you need to do each week.
- Do you or your family members need special clothes for this occasion? Schedule some shopping.

2nd Step: A Week or So Before the Party

CONFIRMATION
Double-check to be sure that all your arrangements are set:

- Confirm details with the caterer, bartender, entertainment, table and tent rental, and housecleaner.

⌀ Check babysitter arrangements.

⌀ Be sure that your special party clothes are ready.

SHOP 'TIL YOU DROP

Swing out to the stores and pick up as much as you can ahead of time. Avoid last-minute store-hopping:

⌀ Buy food, snacks, beverages, and ice.

⌀ Get paper plates, cups, and napkins.

⌀ Purchase decorations.

⌀ Buy film, gifts, wrapping paper, bows, and greeting cards as needed.

PRIORITIES ONLY

You don't have time to turn this into a huge organizing project. Don't sabotage yourself by trying to file the DVDs in perfect order or by cleaning the basement of clutter culprits when your guests won't be going near the basement.

Just concentrate on fixing up the main rooms where you'll be entertaining. What absolutely must be done to get things into shape?

⌀ Foyer, living room, family room:
  • Only if really necessary, wash the windows, wash the carpet, or clean the fireplace.
  • Clean out the coat closet so nothing will pop out and startle your guests.

⌀ Bathrooms:
  • Keep your bathroom really boring by storing personal items in an off-limits room.
  • Put an extra roll of toilet paper where it will easily be found if it is needed.

⌀ Bedrooms:
  • Declutter the one bedroom that will be used to store guests' coats.

⌀ Kitchen and dining room:
  • If necessary, clean the stove and clear out the refrigerator.
  • Iron tablecloths and napkins.

- Start making extra ice cubes.
- Check to be sure plates, glassware, silverware, and bottle opener are spotless and chip free.
- Get out place mats, napkin rings, candles, and a centerpiece.

✐ Basement:

- Declutter areas where guests will be eating, playing games, or dancing.

✐ Outside:

- Put away all gardening items, bikes, and toys, pick up any trash, and scoop the poop.
- Mow the lawn and trim bushes overhanging the sidewalk and porch.
- If necessary, clean the pool.
- If needed, clean the grill and get your barbecue supplies ready.
- Add pots of flowers to the porch or around the backyard.
- Set up the lawn furniture.

3rd Step: The Day Before the Party

DECLUTTER AND CLEAN

Do as much organizing and cleaning as you can the day before the party. Trying to squeeze it all in on the day of the big event is a sure way to kill your party spirit:

✐ Declutter and clean each room:

- Walk into the room, stand there for a second, and look around for eyesores and more of those clutter culprits. Dump the junk in one of your off-limits rooms.
- Straighten everything and empty wastebaskets.
- Dust, sweep, or vacuum.
- Clean the kitchen and bathroom counters and fixtures.
- Tidy the bedroom that will be used for coats.
- Shift some chairs or the coffee table for a better traffic flow.
- If you plan to use the basement or yard, straighten the areas and set up tables.

OVERNIGHT GUESTS

Take a little extra time to be sure these areas are ready for your guests:

- Bathrooms:
  - Put out a full set of towels for each guest. If you only have one bathroom, put their towels in the guest bedroom.
  - Provide soft soap for the sink and shower (bar soap is not hygienic).
  - Have a basket with extra guest supplies on hand, such as new toothbrushes, a small tube of toothpaste, razor, and hand lotion.
  - Add a night-light.
- Bedrooms:
  - Make space in the closet and add extra hangers.
  - Provide empty drawer space.
  - Be sure bed linens are fresh.
  - Provide an extra blanket and pillow.
  - Place a lamp by the bed if there isn't one already there.
  - Put out a box of tissues and a wastebasket.
  - Be sure that you haven't left any personal items around for your guests to discover.
  - Add an alarm clock, radio or TV, fresh flowers, and some magazines.
- Kitchen:
  - Be sure to have some special breakfast treats on hand along with juice and coffee for your overnight guests.

THE FINAL SETUP

The house is picked up and clean. Now you need to turn it into a party place:

- Party mood:
  - Put up all party or holiday decorations.
  - Set out any special gifts, party favors, or photo displays.
  - Arrange flowers and place candles.
- Fine dining:
  - Be sure all dishes are washed and put away.

- Prepare any food that can be fixed ahead of time.
- Set up the table, the buffet or drinks table, and the snack area.
- Put out the coasters and small bowls for nuts and candy.
- Set out wastebaskets with plastic trash liners.

✏ That's entertainment:

- Bring out entertainment items, such as videotapes, DVDs, playing cards, and board games.
- Check that the pool table and Ping-Pong table are cleared and ready for action.
- Set up outdoor games in the backyard.
- Set out CDs or tapes for background music and dancing.
- Have camera, film, and camcorder ready with freshly charged batteries.

4th Step: The Big Day

DON'T PANIC

Now you're ready for the final run-through:

✏ Chow time:

- Finish food preparation or check with the caterers.

✏ Kidding around:

- If your children will be at the party, make sure that they are dressed and ready and have received their good manners reminder.
- Otherwise, take your youngsters to the babysitter's or set them up with snacks and movies in their bedroom.

✏ Check it out:

- Take a quick swing through the whole house to pick up newspapers, toys, and jackets.
- Check that the bathrooms are clean and the coat area is picked up.
- Open the windows to air out the house.
- Adjust the thermostat if necessary.
- Run the vacuum quickly through the main rooms.

✏ Yard work:

- Double-check that the front and backyards look good and that everything is set up if you're having an outdoor party.
- Shift your cars to make room for guest cars.

⬧ Head for the spa:

- Take a nap or a long relaxing bath so that you'll have plenty of pep for the party.
- Give yourself time to dress and get fixed up.

THEY'RE COMING

An hour or so before the party, take care of the following:

⬧ Have one last chat with the caterer, disc jockey, or clown for final details.

⬧ Put your pets in the basement, bedroom, or outside, if necessary.

⬧ Turn on a lamp in the bedroom for coats and a night-light in the bathroom.

⬧ Flip on the porch light.

⬧ Turn on the lights and music in the front room or party area.

⬧ Light the candles, fireplace, or outdoor grill.

⬧ Bring out the ice and beverages for the drinks table and set out snacks.

⬧ Check on the food preparation.

Now, take one last quick look around—then relax, greet your friends, and have fun!

5th Step: The Party's Over

PARTY POOPER

Just do a few basic pickups and put away only the important or perishable things. Retrieve the kids from the babysitter's, then give yourself a break and finish the rest in the morning:

⬧ Put away food and beverages.

⬧ Put dishware in the sink or dishwasher and all trash in the wastebasket.

⬧ Blow out the candles, turn off the lights, and lock up. The party's over.

What's the Final Step?

That was fun. The party was a success. How about some helpful hints for future entertaining? Now it's time to *Set Up a Routine to Control Clutter and Chaos*.

DAILY: Take 20 to 25 Minutes

❑ You remember those clutter culprits? If you've regularly been picking up papers, clothes, food, and toys then you'll just need to do a quick straightening, dusting, and vacuuming to get things in order before guests drop in.

❑ If you entertain a lot, you might consider designating the foyer and living room as off-limits areas that are always ready for guests.

WEEKLY: Take 10 to 15 Minutes

❑ Get some recipes from friends, cookbooks, and magazines. Be prepared to have a selection of tried-and-true recipes so that you can quickly whip up a light lunch, simple dinner, fabulous dessert, or a few tasty snacks and beverages for visitors.

❑ If you've used this party checklist, add any new suggestions that helped things go more smoothly. Check the list to get ready for your next big get-together.

❑ Set aside a small selection of place settings, glasses, and silverware for guests—the ones without any chips, cracks, or water spots.

❑ Keep some cloth or good-quality paper napkins handy.

Chapter 18

PHOTOGRAPHS

Help!

You're a shutterbug. You love taking pictures and you have boxes and boxes of totally unorganized photos. You don't want to turn this into a huge project but you would like to get them into some kind of order. Can you do something about it? It's a snap! Here's the plan.

The First Part of the Plan Is *Schedule It*

Even if your calendar is packed, you can still find a little time each week to dip into those piles of pictures. For example:

- ✎ Watch the news and sort for half an hour each day until you've worked your way through all the pictures.

- ✎ Share the fun. Have a photo-sorting party with your husband, children, sister, or brother.

The Next Part of the Plan Is *Organize It*

The following four steps will help you control your clutter.

1st Step: Sort It Out

GET IT TOGETHER

To begin, let's see what you're dealing with:

- Gather up all the photos and negatives that you can find.
- Put them in a large box. Tape a note to the box and label it PHOTOS TO BE SORTED.
- Leave pictures or negatives in their original store photo package.

SET UP A SYSTEM

Now what? You've got a big box packed with photos. Where do you start? It won't be as confusing as you might think:

- Get another box and label this one PHOTOS TO KEEP. This is where you can store your pictures after they're organized.
- You'll also need a stack of long business envelopes and a pen.
- Grab some envelopes and write a different year on the back of each envelope, such as 2000, 2001, 2002, 2003, 2004, 2005, and 2006. Put the envelopes in your PHOTOS TO KEEP box. Keep them in order by the year.

2nd Step: Organizing Photos

PICTURE PICTURE

This is the fun part. It's no major brain drain, and you don't have to work up a sweat. Just sit and look at photographs:

- Take pictures out of the box of PHOTOS TO BE SORTED and decide whether to keep, dump, or give them away.
- If you have tons of pictures, just grab a small pack, park yourself in front of the TV, and zip through them.

✐ Hey, this picture when you were thirty pounds lighter and actually wearing a two-piece bathing suit—that's a keeper! Drop the picture in the 1995 envelope in your PHOTOS TO KEEP box.

✐ When you run across more 1995 pictures, you know where to file them. If you have a lot of pictures, you may need several envelopes for all the 1995 photos.

✐ If you have a stack of pictures from Christmas 1995 still in the store photo package, quickly pull out the photos you don't want to keep and pop the rest of the package into or next to the 1995 envelope.

✐ Keep going through your pictures and making envelopes for other years as necessary. You may have pictures of your parents or grandparents dating back to the 1940s or earlier.

THE DATING DILEMMA

It's handy to have the date on each picture, but don't worry if you're not sure of the exact month or year:

✐ If the date isn't on the back of the picture or on the store photo package and you're not sure what it is, just take a best guess and pop it into one of the dated envelopes.

✐ You can switch the picture around later if you finally get a fix on the year.

DUMP OR GIVE AWAY

Can't bear to throw away a single one of your pictures? Really, you don't need to keep every single photo that you ever took.

How do you tell the difference between the keepers and the stuff to toss? As you sort through your photos, set up the following two piles:

✐ Definitely dump:
  • That picture of you in this year's bathing suit must *never* be seen again.
  • Your family and friends look really awful.
  • The picture is fuzzy and unfocused.
  • It's too dark or too light to see details.
  • You can't tell who or what is in the picture.

- You have a dozen pictures of the same thing. Just keep a couple of the best ones; put the others in the give-away pile.

✐ Give away:

- If you have extra pictures, offer them to family and friends.

INFO OVERLOAD

Without any information, you're wondering, "Who the heck is that person I'm standing next to?" Plus, you don't have a clue where that lake or beautiful ruin or cathedral is located:

✐ As you're sorting, you might want to quickly write the date, name, and subject on the back of each picture. If that idea gives you a headache then don't bother with it.

✐ However, it is worth it to think about labeling them. You could do a few at a time while you're watching TV. (Be sure not to press too hard as you write on the back of the photo and make sure the ink is dry so it won't smear.)

✐ At the very least, take the time to list brief contents on the outside of each store photo package. At a glance, you'll know exactly what's in each package. For instance:
  2002—September
  Chris and Bill's wedding
  Trees in backyard—fall colors
  New puppy

DIGITAL CAMERAS AND COMPUTER DISKS

Do you need to set up a separate photo system?

✐ If you have your film processed onto disks, memory cards, or flash drives, label them and store them in a box.

✐ Set up a folder to save photo proof sheets.

✐ You might want to transfer all of your digital images from your computer to an external hard drive to free up space on your computer.

3rd Step: Negatives

ACCENTUATE THE NEGATIVE

Don't worry too much about getting your negatives in perfect order. You can get good copies of photos, without a negative, at the local copying store:

- If you find negatives with your wedding or graduation pictures, put them in a separate envelope and list the date and contents.
- File the envelopes by date in a box marked NEGATIVES.
- If you have a big jumble of negatives, just stick them in an envelope and put them in the NEGATIVES box.
- Store your negatives on a different floor than your photos or, if possible, at a friend's house. Then if something happens to some of your pictures, such as damage from a flood or fire, you'll still have the negatives.
- Don't keep negatives or photos in a safe-deposit box. It may damage them.

4th Step: Photo Storage

PHOTO FINISH

You've sorted all your photos, computer disks, and negatives. What if you don't have the time, money, or interest in putting together photo albums or scrapbooks?

- No problem. The pictures in your PHOTOS TO KEEP box are in envelopes and are filed by the year. They may not be in an album but they're all in one spot and easy to find.
- The photos may not be in perfect order but at least you know that you can find your Hawaiian vacation pictures somewhere in the 1999 envelope and your parents' fiftieth wedding anniversary pictures in the 1987 envelope.
- When you get new photos, just pop them in the box by the date and you're done.
- Keep your photos in any kind of box, such as a shoebox, plastic box, or special photo box.

- If you end up with several boxes of photos, label each box—for example, Photos 1990–1999.
- Store your boxes of photos in a safe place. Don't leave them near heat, bright light, water, or where little kids can get into them.

PICTURE PERFECT

If you're planning to put the pictures in photo albums or scrapbooks, your photos are ready and waiting in your PHOTOS TO KEEP box:

- Options for organizing your pictures:
  - Placing them in straight chronological order works just fine.
  - Create a special album for each of your children.
  - Why not have a whole album with pictures of your pets?
  - Set up separate albums for weddings, vacations, or new babies.
  - Here's a chance to be creative. You can trim and rearrange pictures and add all kinds of decorative and personal touches in a scrapbook, such as the ticket stub from your favorite play or a matchbook and napkin from that special night out on the town.
- Label the outside of each album and scrapbook.
- Be sure to store them where they will be protected.

What's the Final Step?

It feels great to have your photos in order. How can you avoid future picture pileups? Now it's time to *Set Up a Routine to Control Clutter and Chaos*.

DAILY: Take 5 Minutes

❑ Got a picture of your grandson or a packet of Christmas photos? Quickly write the date, name, and subject on the back of each photo.

❑ Pop all new pictures into the TO DO—PHOTOS envelope with your current TO DO folders.

WEEKLY: Take 3 to 5 Minutes

❑ After you pay your bills, file new photos, by date, in your PHO-TOS TO KEEP box.

❑ Delete unwanted pictures from the camera memory card, then transfer the remaining photos to the computer.

MONTHLY: Take 15 Minutes

❑ Hum along with your new CD or enjoy a TV sitcom while you're adding new pictures to your photo albums or scrapbooks.

❑ Edit and print photos or save photos onto a flash drive.

Chapter 19

TRAVEL AIDS

~~~~~~~~~~~~~~~~~~

Help!

Is getting ready for a trip usually a big hassle? Do you have to go on a safari around the house trying to find passports, guidebooks, flight bags, and suitcase keys? Can you do something about it? Absolutely! Here's the plan.

The First Part of the Plan Is *Schedule It*

Don't have any immediate travel plans? Great. Now's the perfect time to get your travel items together and shipshape. For example:

- Break your project down into a few quick steps. Take a little time Friday after dinner to start rounding up all travel papers and luggage.
- Do you have an hour on Saturday to set up a shelf for travel books, maps, and brochures as well as a folder for official travel papers?

The Next Part of the Plan Is *Organize It*

The following three steps will help you control your clutter.

1st Step: Inventory

ROUND 'EM UP

First, let's find out what you have and get it together:

- Gather up your official travel documents, such as passports and frequent flyer paperwork.
- Next, stack all your travel brochures and magazine and newspaper articles together.
- Find your necessary travel items, such as luggage, travel alarm, and small plastic bottles.

MOVE 'EM OUT

You can accumulate quite a collection of flight bags and travel items that actually have never been on a trip with you. It's time for a little sorting:

- If you'd like, save your old passports as travel mementos. However, get rid of those clutter culprits, such as old health records, past airline information, and outdated travel brochures, maps, and articles.
- Throw out luggage and travel bags that are torn, have damaged handles, or have broken wheels that can't be fixed.
- Maybe it's time to part with the luggage you received for your high school graduation thirty years ago.
- Do you have five fanny packs but seldom even use one of them? Offer some to friends or donate them.
- Dump plastic travel bottles that are stained or cracked.
- Test your old travel alarm, travel iron, shaver, and curling iron to be sure that they still work.

2nd Step: Travelogue

TRAVEL LIBRARY

Set up a convenient spot for current travel plans and information:

- File travel books, guidebooks, and world-language phrase books together.
- Set up an ACTION folder with current vacation plans and include:
  - Tickets
  - Letters, bills, and confirmations from the travel agent, airlines, hotels, and resorts
  - Travel catalogs, brochures, articles, maps, website travel lists, discount coupons, currency chart, and list of world-language phrases
  - Recommendations from friends for places to visit
- After your trip, either file items or throw them away.

TRIPPING

Set up another spot in your home office or basement for storing travel documents, vacation mementos, and travel ideas:

- Set up a folder for travel documents and important information. Keep it in a file cabinet with your PERMANENT BUSINESS AND HOUSEHOLD folders and include the following items:
  - Copy of your passport (store your actual passport in a safe-deposit box)
  - Frequent flyer cards and train-pass information
  - Health certificate with required vaccinations for world travel
  - Small envelope with all suitcase keys
  - Small amounts of foreign currency in envelopes
  - Lists of the names and addresses of the members of past tour groups
  - Lists of hotels and restaurants that you might like to visit again
  - Names of contacts at travel agencies who were helpful
- Save mementos from past travels:
  - Create scrapbooks with photos, picture postcards, articles, brochures, maps, shipboard newsletters, and ticket stubs.
  - Store clothing, decorative items, and other trip mementos in a separate box.

✐ Keep a folder for future trip ideas in your PERSONAL INTER-EST folders and include:

- Travel articles, pictures, and brochures for places you'd like to visit
- Maps, lists of travel websites, and articles with travel tips

3rd Step: Have Bag, Will Travel

BAG IT

Choose one spot to store all your luggage and travel items:

✐ Place all your smaller travel bags—carry-on, tote bag, flight bag, fanny pack, knapsack, special travel purse, document wallet, and money belt—inside a couple of clear plastic trash bags.

✐ Keep the plastic bags right next to your luggage or, if possible, store them inside the larger suitcases.

✐ Place special travel items, such as a travel alarm clock and travel iron, into a small plastic bag and store them inside a larger suitcase.

PACK IT IN

When you're packing for a trip, don't just toss everything into your suitcase. Organize with smaller bags so that you can find things more quickly:

✐ Select two large purse-size bags for storing personal items. Place all your grooming supplies and cosmetics in one bag and all hair-care items, including hair blower and curling iron, in the other bag.

✐ When you travel, leave the two bags on the bathroom counter in the hotel. Everything will be conveniently and neatly in one spot. No more clutter scattered around the room.

✐ Never take large bottles that are full. Buy small travel-size products or fill smaller plastic bottles with shampoo, cleansing lotion, and moisturizer.

✐ Use lots of little bags to help organize your suitcase. Buy cloth or plastic travel bags or even gallon-size freezer bags. Use see-through bags so that you can spot what you need and grab it faster.

✎ Little bags can really come in handy for containing the following items and more:

- Medication
- Grooming supplies
- Cosmetics
- Grooming items and cosmetics that could leak
- Jewelry
- Sewing kit
- Underwear
- Damp clothing
- Soiled clothing
- All the little pieces of paper and brochures you collect each day
- Stamps and picture postcards you plan to send or to keep
- Film
- Batteries
- Gum, mints, and candy
- Food
- Trash

What's the Final Step?

The next time the travel bug strikes, you'll be ready. No more sending out search parties to look for your passport, travel alarm clock, and fanny pack. Now it's time to *Set Up a Routine to Control Clutter and Chaos*.

DAILY: Take a Couple of Minutes

❏ If you buy a travel guidebook or map, file it on your travel shelf.

❏ Store any new luggage or travel gear with your other luggage.

WEEKLY: Take 5 to 10 Minutes

❑ Take a few minutes to clip interesting travel articles and pop them into your TRAVEL folder.

Chapter 20

TRAVEL PLANS

Help!

How about all that racing around trying to make your travel plans at the last minute? Do you start your vacations tired and cranky? Can you do something about it? But of course! Here's the plan.

The First Part of the Plan Is *Schedule It*

You're ready to do some serious traveling. A little advanced planning can start you out relaxed and ready to enjoy your vacation. For example:

- Use the checklists in this chapter to help you get ready for your trip. A more detailed checklist of items to pack is outlined in Chapter 21.
- Take a couple of afternoons and start making phone calls, visiting websites, or checking with your travel agent to set up arrangements.

✐ Make a series of quick stops after work to get your required vaccinations and to pick up traveler's checks, medication, film, and maybe a couple of new outfits.

The Next Part of the Plan Is *Organize It*

The following four steps will help make your vacation great.

1st Step: Advanced Planning

BUSINESS TRIPS

Double-check everything so that your business trip runs smoothly:

✐ Confirm travel and lodging arrangements.

✐ Confirm times and locations for appointments and meetings.

✐ Prepare your speech, reports, and handouts.

✐ If you travel regularly, have a suitcase or overnight bag packed with basic grooming and cosmetic supplies plus a fresh set of underwear and pajamas.

✐ If you're a frequent flyer, store your passport and important travel papers together in a special travel wallet or belt.

✐ Keep your briefcase ready for business trips and stocked with basic office supplies.

FAMILY AND HOUSEHOLD

Avoid last-minute decisions and hassles. Figure out what needs to be done and take care of it ahead of time:

✐ Arrange for childcare and pet care while you're gone.

✐ Arrange for newspapers and mail to be held or to be picked up by a neighbor.

✐ Ask a neighbor to keep an eye on your place for packages or problems and perhaps to water your yard.

- If necessary, cancel your yard and pool service.
- Consider notifying the local police department of the dates that you will be gone.
- Arrange for the storage of valuables.
- Decide what clothes you will need to take based on the climate and your planned activities. Inspect the items carefully to make sure they are clean, with no buttons missing, and zippers in working order. Take them to the cleaners or tailor at least a week before your departure.
- Decide which suitcases and carry-on bags you'll be taking.

FINANCIAL PLANNER

You won't get too far without plenty of paper or plastic:

- Decide how much money you'll need and which credit and debit cards to take.
- If necessary, purchase a small amount of foreign money.
- Make a copy of a foreign currency chart that you can put in your wallet.

TRAVEL BUG

Take a few precautions so that you'll have a healthy trip:

- Renew your prescriptions. Plan to take extra medical supplies.
- Check with your doctor about a prescription for motion-sickness pills or for special earache medication if you will be flying with children.
- Take a list of all the medications you use and information about any current health concerns, such as diabetes or high blood pressure.
- Call the local world travel health clinic. Find out what vaccinations are required.

TRIP OUT

Don't wait until the last minute to make these important arrangements:

- Purchase your travel tickets.
- Make hotel and resort reservations.

- Renew your passport, if necessary.
- When traveling with children in a foreign country be sure that you have their birth certificates. If you are divorced, carry all legal custody papers when crossing borders.
- Place an order for special meals on the plane.
- Check ahead to see what childcare facilities and services are available on planes and in hotels.
- Find out about pet policies.
- Keep all letters confirming flights, train seats, tours, hotel rooms, and restaurants and take them with you on the trip. If you have booked over the Internet, be sure to print out the confirmations immediately and place them in a folder.
- Arrange for transportation to the airport or train station.

ON THE ROAD AGAIN

Save yourself some travel headaches by first making sure that your vehicle is in good working order:

- Check car or van fluids, tires, and brakes before your road trip.
- Be sure that you have protective car seats for children and that all the seat and shoulder belts work.

ADIOS, I'M ON MY WAY

You can't just disappear for a week or two. Don't forget to notify the people who need to know you'll be gone:

- Mention your vacation plans to your family members, boss, co-workers, children's school, team, or club.
- Rearrange appointments and handle special projects at work before you leave.
- Have your kids get assignments from their teachers.
- Arrange for a substitute for your bowling team or reschedule the days that you volunteer.
- Check your calendar and if necessary, change hair and dentist appointments.

2nd Step: Only One Week Left

FINAL ARRANGEMENTS

Go over this checklist to be sure that all the important arrangements are confirmed and that you have all your travel supplies:

- Check that you've got your tickets, passports, and health certificates for international travel.
- Confirm all reservations and travel plans. Confirm details, such as a nonsmoking room, balcony, or suite and if pets are allowed.
- Confirm all home arrangements for children, pets, mail, and newspapers.
- Leave an extra set of house and car keys, security alarm information, and a list of hotels and travel details with a relative or friend.
- Pick up your traveler's checks and all of your travel money.
- Buy film and batteries.
- Pick up an extra supply of prescription medications and motion sickness remedies.
- Lock jewelry, extra cash, diary, and important business papers in a file cabinet or safe.

3rd Step: Vacation Getaway

FINAL CHECK

It never hurts to check one more time before you head on out for fun. Remember, the family forgot their son, Kevin, in the movie *Home Alone*:

- If there's a question about weather, call ahead to check on conditions.
- Take the children to the babysitter and pets to the petsitter.
- Toss out (or give to a neighbor) milk, fruit, vegetables, and anything that could spoil. Take out the trash.
- Unplug major appliances.
- Adjust the thermometer to a lower temperature in the winter and be sure to turn off the air-conditioning in the summer.

- Turn off the washing machine faucets.

- Lock all vehicles that will be left at home. Don't leave any valuable items in the vehicles or in the garage.

- Make sure that the water hoses have been turned off.

- Take a last check that you have your tickets, passport, health certificate, driver's license, money, credit cards, insurance card, medicine, eyeglasses, and keys.

- Double-check that you have all your luggage, including carry-on and tote bag.

- Turn off all the lights except for the lights on timers.

- Be sure that all the windows and doors are locked and the security alarm is set.

4th Step: Puttin' on the Ritz

MAID SERVICE

Let's put it all together now and start your vacation off right. When you get to your hotel, motel, or cottage, first relax and enjoy the view, then take a moment to get a little organized:

- Place your two small bags with grooming and hair-care items on the bathroom counter and leave them there.

- Hang up your clothes and put a few things in one or two drawers.

- Set your alarm clock to the current local time and place it and your book next to the bed.

- Store your luggage and purse out of sight in the closet.

- Consider storing your valuables in the hotel or room safe.

- With everything out of sight, you can sit back and enjoy a room that looks attractive and makes you feel like you're someplace special.

- When your things are in only a few spots, it's a breeze to gather them up quickly and be on your way. You can head on down the highway without worrying that you forgot something.

What's the Final Step?

Ready! Set! Go! Take a little time to get organized so you can start your trip relaxed and in the mood for fun. Now it's time to *Set Up a Routine to Control Clutter and Chaos*.

DAILY: Take 10 to 15 Minutes

❑ As you plan your trip, keep all tickets, itinerary, and travel information in your TRAVEL folder.

❑ Keep a TO DO list in the folder. Jot down any questions or things you need to take care of before your trip.

❑ Set up a spot for items you bought for the trip, such as film, motion-sickness pills, hat, and sandals.

WEEKLY: Take 10 to 15 Minutes

❑ Each Sunday check the lists in this chapter. Figure out what you still have to do and make your plans for the week.

Chapter 21

TRAVEL CHECKLIST

Help!

You travel a lot and end up either hauling around a whole bunch of stuff you don't need or frequently forgetting important things. Can you do something about it? No problemo! Here's the plan.

The First Part of the Plan Is *Schedule It*

This is the week you're heading out on your big trip. It's time to start packing it in. Use the checklists in this chapter to help you. For example:

- ✐ A couple of days before you leave take time after dinner to pack everything in the suitcases except your clothes.
- ✐ Set aside time to iron and organize your travel clothes.
- ✐ The night before your trip, get your purse, wallet, money belt, and carry-on organized.
- ✐ At this point fold and pack your clothes.

The Next Part of the Plan Is *Organize It*

The following two steps will help you control your clutter.

1st Step: Carry-On, Wallet, Money Belt

CARRY-ON

Keep basic survival items in your carry-on in case your luggage goes off in a different direction than you do. Include the following, but keep in mind that some items may be barred due to national security concerns:

- Medication, eyeglasses, and contacts
- Feminine hygiene and birth-control products
- Travel toothbrush and toothpaste
- Shaving supplies, deodorant, and hand cream
- Cosmetics, comb, and brush
- Tissues and a small roll of toilet paper
- Valuable jewelry
- Set of underwear
- Cell phone, camera, film
- Computer with case
- Necessary childcare items

WALLET

Travel with a light wallet. Never keep your main money sources, identification, or important papers in your wallet:

- Small amount of cash
- Two or three traveler's checks
- Small foreign currency conversion chart

MONEY BELT

Always keep the most important things in your money belt. If your purse, wallet, or carry-on is lost or stolen, you can still have a shot at enjoying your trip. Include the following items:

- Passport and tickets
- Cash, credit cards, debit card, and traveler's checks
- Frequent flyer card and hotel discount card
- Driver's license and auto and health insurance cards
- If necessary, children's birth certificates and custody papers
- Itinerary with a list of your tour hotels and phone numbers
- List of your prescription medications and your physician's name and phone number
- Emergency contact and phone number
- House key, car key, and luggage keys (leave the rest of your keys at home)

2nd Step: Pack Your Bags

PACKING LIST

You obviously can't take everything on this list unless you're using a U-Haul. Use the following packing list to help remind you of what you might need on your trips. Feel free to ignore or add any items.

In order to pass airport security, be sure that you don't have any questionable items, such as a nail file or sewing kit, in your purse or carry-on bag.

Business Travel

- Tickets
- Corporate travel plan and agenda
- Hotel discount cards
- Phone list of car rental, limousine service, and travel agent
- Cell phone and list of important business phone numbers
- Business cards
- Envelopes, stamps, and stationery
- Envelope for all receipts
- Laptop computer and supplies
- Calculator and electronic calendar
- Notebook and pens
- Papers to be signed, speech to be delivered, reports, and handouts

⊘ Folder for each company, client, project, or territory

⊘ Appropriate clothing for your business trip, including clothes for travel, meetings, sports, casual dinners, and formal parties

Baby Care

⊘ Bottles, formula, baby food, plate, cup, baby spoon, and bibs

⊘ Washcloths and towels

⊘ Diapers, wipe cloths, powder, lotion, and disposal bag

⊘ Baby shampoo and soap

⊘ Blanket

⊘ Baby knapsack or carrier

⊘ Crib and stroller

⊘ Rattles and toys

Health

⊘ Prescription medications

⊘ Nonprescription medications for headaches, indigestion, allergies

⊘ Motion-sickness remedies

⊘ Children's medications

⊘ Medical alert bracelet

⊘ Small first-aid kit

⊘ Sunscreen

⊘ Insect repellent

⊘ Sanitizing gel and hand wipes

Personal Care

⊘ Hair care:
  • Brush, comb, shampoo, rinse, hair blower, and curling iron
  • Hair spray, hair gel, and hair ornaments

⊘ Skin care:
  • Facial soap and moisturizer, astringent, cotton balls, and facial mask
  • Hand and body soap and moisturizer and deodorant

- Electrical shaver or razor, shaving cream, and after-shave lotion
- Tweezers

⌀ Eyes, ears, and nose:
- Contacts, extra pair, solutions, and washer
- Eyeglasses, extra pair, reading glasses, and sunglasses
- Eyedrops and eye-makeup remover
- Ear swabs and hearing aid
- Tissues and nasal spray

⌀ Mouth:
- Dental floss, lip balm, and mouthwash
- Toothbrush and toothpaste/powder

⌀ Hands and feet:
- Nail clippers and file, nail polish, and polish remover
- Hands and body lotion
- Pumice stone, moleskin, and shoe padding

Personal Items
⌀ Feminine hygiene products

⌀ Birth-control supplies

⌀ Roll of toilet paper

Cosmetics
⌀ Eye shadow, eyebrow pencil, eyeliner, mascara, and brushes

⌀ Lipstick, lip liner, and gloss

⌀ Liquid makeup, pancake makeup, and touch-up

⌀ Rouge and dusting powder

⌀ Cologne and perfume

⌀ Small stand-up mirror

Clothes, Accessories, and Shoes
⌀ Underwear

⌀ Nightwear

⌀ Casual clothes and shoes

⌀ Informal social occasion clothes and shoes

⌀ Evening and special events clothes and shoes

- Formal evening clothes and shoes
- Sports and exercise clothes and shoes
- Beachwear and thongs
- Children's clothes and shoes
- Hats, gloves, and scarves
- Jackets and coats
- Watch and jewelry
- Small sewing kit
- Soap for washing clothes and travel hangers
- Travel iron

Entertainment and Recreation

- Gifts and pictures for family and friends that you'll be visiting
- Books and magazines to read
- Playing cards and travel board games such as chess and checkers
- Dolls, robots, and toys
- Frisbee and softball
- Musical instruments, such as a guitar
- Sketchbook, pencils, and art supplies
- Camera, film, flash attachment, photo printer, film protective bag, and extra camera battery
- Camcorder and batteries
- Sports equipment, including golf clubs and tennis racket
- Beach blanket, towels, chairs, umbrella, water toys, and floating mats
- Picnic basket, dishes, cooler, can opener, and blanket
- Small radio, CD player, and selection of CDs
- Camping and hiking equipment
- Hunting and fishing equipment

Travel Aids

- Battery-operated travel alarm clock
- Adapter and converter for world travel

- Binoculars
- Flashlight
- Folding paper fan to block sun and to work up a little breeze
- Hat and umbrella for protection from the rain and the sun
- Inflatable neck and back pillows
- Eyeshades and earplugs
- Nylon expandable bag for carrying souvenirs home
- Guidebooks, maps, and world-language dictionary or phrase book
- Notebook and pens
- Stationery, envelopes, and stamps
- Addresses of family and friends
- Cell phone and charger

Vehicles

- Emergency supplies, including a flashlight, first-aid kit, flares, empty gas can, windshield wiper fluid, can of oil, tarp, bag of sand or kitty litter for winter travel, shovel, window scraper, tools, axe, rope, a jack, and a spare tire
- Pack a cooler and tote bag with bottles of water, soft drinks, fruits, and snacks
- Tissues, paper towels, moist towels, trash bags, and wastebasket
- Plastic box or bag with kids' games, toys, crayons and coloring books, travel checkers and chess sets, playing cards, crossword puzzles, word searches, books, and magazines
- Selection of tape cassettes and CDs
- Selection of videotapes or DVDs
- Travel organizer to hang over the back of the front seat for books, games, and toys
- Pillow and blanket for each passenger
- Pet supplies if your pets are traveling with you

What's the Final Step?

Always use these checklists to help you pack. Otherwise, you'll be set-tling in on the plane for your next trip and suddenly remember: "Oh, no! Did I forget that again?" Now it's time to *Set Up a Routine to Control Clutter and Chaos*.

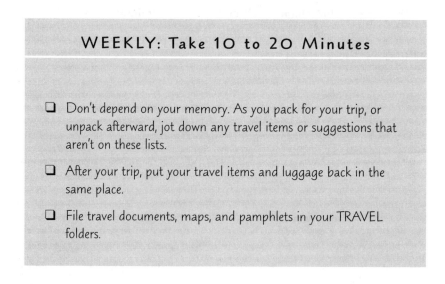

WEEKLY: Take 10 to 20 Minutes

❑ Don't depend on your memory. As you pack for your trip, or unpack afterward, jot down any travel items or suggestions that aren't on these lists.

❑ After your trip, put your travel items and luggage back in the same place.

❑ File travel documents, maps, and pamphlets in your TRAVEL folders.

Part Three

ANKLE-DEEP
CLUTTER AND CHAOS

What's been happening up to this point? So far, maybe you've tackled some of the knee-deep clutter, conquered those clutter culprits, set up an In-and-Out Shelf, and reorganized your calendar.

Did you jump into some of your hip-deep clutter? Maybe you sorted your paper overload, fixed up the basement, and organized a few other hot spots. You've turned a lot of your uncontrollable clutter into controllable clutter.

Has it been worth the effort? Ask yourself, "What do I want my life to be like?" Isn't it a lot nicer to start each day smoothly without racing around trying to find work and school materials? Don't you enjoy coming home, opening the door, and not facing another big mess? Isn't it great not having to waste time hunting for bills and business papers? Now that your clothes and entertainment items are organized, isn't it a relief not having to wade through a bunch of stuff? Isn't it delightful to have a little more time to relax and enjoy yourself?

If the answer is yes then let's figure out your next step. If you're like me, you hate that sense of panic when you can't find something, when you're always running around at the last minute, and when your piles of junk and things to do are as high as an elephant's eye.

Let's pull it all together and set up some DAILY and WEEKLY ROUTINES to help you maintain an attractive home with normal, manageable, ankle-deep clutter.

Chapter 22

THE DAILY AND WEEKLY ROUTINES

Help! I don't want to do it!

Have you peeked ahead at the lists of DAILY and WEEKLY ROUTINES? Did you say, "I don't think so. I can't do all that every day. I don't want to do it!"

Here's the deal. First, I'm not talking about waxing baseboards and alphabetizing spices. We're just concerned with clutter culprits and the basics for maintaining a normal home. Eventually, you're going to have to wash those dishes, clean your clothes, pay the bills, and mow the lawn. Why not plan for it? Why not work these chores into a daily part of your life?

Second, be realistic. Will you still have some messy rooms? Yup! Will you still occasionally misplace things? You bet. There will always be times when you lose it. You'll be knee-deep and even hip-deep in uncontrollable clutter and chaos.

That's when the DAILY and WEEKLY ROUTINES can help you turn uncontrollable clutter into ankle-deep, controllable clutter. Take a deep breath and get yourself back on track. Clear up your problems by following the plan.

The First Part of the Plan Is *Schedule It*

Don't try this during the week that your daughter is getting married, your first grandchild is due, and the final draft of your company's annual report has to be on the boss's desk by 10:00 a.m. on Friday:

- Check your calendar and decide that this is the week to get started.
- Make a copy of the DAILY ROUTINE at the end of this chapter and tape it to the refrigerator or keep it on your desk.

The Next Part of the Plan Is *Organize It*

You are not expected to do everything on the first day. Stick a toe into the water first:

- Start following only the morning routine for a couple of days until it feels like an easy and comfortable habit.
- Add the coming-home routines and then the evening routines by the end of the week; turn them into daily habits that are on autopilot.
- Use the weekly checklist to help you add cleaning, clothes care, yard work, and bill-paying to your WEEKLY ROUTINE.
- Each Sunday look over your YEARLY CHECKLIST, which will be discussed in Chapter 23, to see what activities and responsibilities need to be handled that month.

What's the Final Step?

We can't postpone it any longer. Here we go. Now it's time to *Set Up a Routine to Control Clutter and Chaos*.

Use the following eight tips to help you figure out easy ways to squeeze in daily and weekly chores.

Tips List

1. Couch Potatoes Arise: Instead of taking a block of time to do chores, hop up and do some quick straightening or cleaning during several commercials:

   ⊘ Zip around with the kids and pick up toys during a TV break.

   ⊘ The daily kitchen cleanup won't be so tedious if you do it in spurts:
   - 1st Break: Put all food away
   - 2nd Break: Clear the table
   - 3rd Break: Scrape the plates and load the dishwasher
   - 4th Break: Wipe the table and counter
   - 5th Break: Rinse and put cans and bottles in the recycling bin
   - 6th Break: Pack lunches for the next day

   ⊘ If you love your TV programs you can actually finish most of your weekly housecleaning during commercial breaks:
   - 1st Break: Straighten up the bathroom
   - 2nd Break: Clean the toilet
   - 3rd Break: Clean the bathroom sink
   - 4th Break: Straighten up the living room
   - 5th Break: Dust
   - 6th Break: Vacuum half of the living room
   - 7th Break: Vacuum the rest of the room

2. Divide and Conquer: If you hate the weekly grind of housecleaning and the idea of huge projects such as spring gardening or taxes stops you cold, it might help to break up those big chores into smaller projects:

   ⊘ Sweep the porch, deck, and sidewalks on Thursday. Pick up toys, pet deposits, and trash on Saturday.

   ⊘ Buy Christmas cards on Monday, address and stamp envelopes on Thursday, and write messages and sign your name on Sunday.

⊘ Spring gardening breakdown:
- Day 1: Trim all your bushes and trees
- Day 2: Rake the leaves
- Day 3: Buy grass seed, topsoil, and plants
- Day 4: Add topsoil and put in new plants
- Day 5: Plant grass seed
- Day 6: Bring out the deck and yard furniture
- Day 7: Rest!

⊘ Income tax breakdown:
- February: Gather up all the tax papers

⊘ March: The first week work on your federal taxes

⊘ March: The second week work on your state taxes

⊘ March: The third week prepare your final copies or take them to the tax office

3. Half-and-Half: You don't always have to finish a big project in one day. Break it down into two sets of chores:

⊘ Take an hour or so on Thursday to dust and vacuum the rooms on the main floor. Friday after work take care of the rooms on the second floor.

⊘ Give the house a really major cleaning one week. The next week do a minor cleaning in half the time. Quickly spruce up the bathrooms, and give the main rooms a fast dust and vacuum.

⊘ Pay bills one day and work on business and household papers another day.

⊘ Tackle half of the basement this weekend and finish the other half next weekend.

4. Just Do It: If all else fails, sometimes it's best to just do it and get it over with:

⊘ You're already in the bedroom, bathroom, or kitchen. Instead of facing a mess when you return home, take a few minutes and immediately put things back where they belong.

⊘ When you come home after work, take a half hour or so to zip through the mail, answer messages, check your calendar, and put new items away. Then you're done with it.

- It's Memorial Day weekend. A lot of people get 90 percent of their spring gardening done over these three days.

- Automatically end each day with a quick pickup before you lock up.

- Set aside a block of time, such as a Wednesday evening, for paying your bills and taking care of your business papers.

- Plan on one horrendous weekend in March and just do your income taxes.

5. Multitask: You don't have to face a blank wall and grimly work on a chore. There are lots of projects you can do and enjoy yourself at the same time:

    - Park yourself in front of the TV and organize your purse, put new photos in an album, and set up your weekly medications.

    - Turn on some lively music and clean out a messy drawer or straighten up the CD pile.

    - Sort, fold, and iron the laundry while chatting with your kids or watching a movie.

    - Straighten the garage while you're listening to a ball game.

6. Outsource: There's nothing that says you have to do everything yourself. Go ahead and get some help:

    - Pay a neighbor kid to mow the lawn and shovel snow.

    - Hire someone to clean your house every other week.

    - Get a professional in to clean the carpet, to paint the kitchen, or even to help you organize your papers and folders.

7. Share the Fun: If you share your home with others be sure to share the workload:

    - Encourage pride in your home. When you're having company, everyone pitches in to make the place look great.

    - As the kids get old enough, they can make their own breakfast and lunch; wash dishes; handle a dust rag, broom, and vacuum cleaner; and help out with weeding, watering, mowing, and shoveling snow.

✏ Divvy up chores fairly between yourself and your significant other. Each may pick the chores that he or she prefers to do. If it turns out that you both hate yard work, get out there as a team and rake the leaves or trim the bushes. Then plop on the couch and enjoy a movie together.

✏ Get the family out for a fall Saturday afternoon of trimming and raking, and don't forget about storing the deck furniture before the first snowfall. Then have hamburgers and French fries for everyone.

8. Take a 10-Minute Computer or Project Break: Stand up, get your circulation going, and squeeze in a few chores:

✏ Take some breaks from the paper you're preparing for work:

- 1st Break: Get your clothes ready for the next day.
- 2nd Break: Make lunches and put your work papers and items for errands on the In-and-Out Shelf.

✏ Take a break from your art or woodworking project and answer a few e-mails or phone messages.

When you put your DAILY and WEEKLY ROUTINES on autopilot, you might discover that you're now totally unable to drop a jacket on the floor or leave snacks on the sofa. Nope, you just can't do it. You'll automatically take thirty seconds to hang up that jacket and one minute to return those snacks to the kitchen.

Remember, you don't have to be perfect. Just keep following the DAILY and WEEKLY ROUTINES and aim for a pleasant, comfortable, and reasonably organized home with no clutter culprits in sight.

Best wishes. You can do it!

The Daily Routine

Use this checklist to help you control clutter and chaos. Skip those projects that you're not interested in and add your own suggestions as needed.

Good Morning: Stop the Clutter Cycle!

1ST STEP: BATHROOM BUFFING (TAKE 5 EXTRA MINUTES)

- Shower (or in the evening).
- Shave, fix hair, and apply makeup.
- Hang up towels and robe or toss in the hamper.
- Wipe up hair and toothpaste globs.
- Toss tissues and cotton balls in the wastebasket.
- Put away all products and equipment.
- Turn off the light.

2ND STEP: BEDROOM BEAUTIFICATION (TAKE 5 TO 10 EXTRA MINUTES)

- Get dressed.
- Hang up clothes or put them back in drawers.
- Make the bed.
- Open curtains and turn off the light.

3RD STEP: KP DUTY AND SPOT PATROL (TAKE 5 TO 10 MINUTES)

- Put away food.
- Prepare a bag lunch (unless you fixed it the previous night).
- Place dirty dishes in the sink or dishwasher.
- Wipe table, countertop, and stove.
- Dump trash into the trash can.
- Turn off all appliances and lights.

4TH STEP: HEAD 'EM UP, MOVE 'EM OUT (TAKE 5 MINUTES)

- Pick up lunch or lunch money.
- Get keys, purse, wallet, and checkbook.
- Do you need an umbrella, jacket, gloves, or boots?
- Check the In-and-Out Shelf for work and school items.

⬤ Be sure pets are inside.

⬤ Turn off lights, set the security alarm, and lock up.

TIPS: You can make the above routines a little easier if you use the suggestions in the Tips List. Consider using the Just Do It tip every morning.

Good Afternoon: Stop Creeping Clutter!

1ST STEP: IT STOPS RIGHT HERE (TAKE 15 TO 30 MINUTES)

⬤ Drop off items on the In-and-Out Shelf.

⬤ Hang up coat, put hat and gloves away, and line up shoes.

⬤ Put groceries away.

⬤ Put other purchases away later when you have time.

2ND STEP: KEEP IN TOUCH (TAKE 5 TO 15 MINUTES)

⬤ Check your answering machine, e-mail, and fax messages and return only the most important ones.

⬤ Sort mail, dump it, or put it into folders.

⬤ Stack magazines, newspapers, and catalogs.

⬤ Check the calendar to see what's scheduled for the next day.

⬤ Get items ready for the following day.

TIPS: Consider using the Couch Potatoes Arise tip and check your calendar during a commercial; Just Do It and answer e-mails; Multitask and sort mail while watching TV; and Take a 10-Minute Computer or Project Break and open new purchases and put them away.

Good Evening: Conquer the Chaos!

1ST STEP: KP DUTY AND SPOT PATROL—AGAIN (TAKE 10 TO 15 MINUTES)

⬤ Put food away and wipe table, counter, and stove.

⬤ Wash dishes.

⬤ Put trash into the trash can and cans and bottles into the recycling bins.

⬤ Prepare next-day lunches if necessary.

2ND STEP: PLAN AHEAD
(TAKE 10 TO 15 MINUTES)

- Get clothes ready for the next day.
- Place items on the In-and-Out Shelf, including school and work materials, letters to be mailed, coupons, and videotapes to return.
- Remind family members of upcoming plans.

3RD STEP: CLOSING UP SHOP
(TAKE 10 MINUTES)

- Walk through the house quickly straightening things; toss paper in the trash.
- After washing, hang up towels and put away grooming products.
- Hang up clothes or put them in the clothes hamper.
- Check to be sure that the kids and pets are OK.
- Lock up the doors and windows and set the security alarm.

TIPS: Consider using the Couch Potatoes Arise tip to clean the kitchen and make lunches; Just Do It and follow your lockup routine; Multitask and get clothes ready while listening to music; Share the Fun and have your children help pick up their toys; and Take a 10-Minute Computer or Project Break to straighten up the house and put items on the In-and-Out Shelf.

The Weekly Routine

Use this checklist to help you control clutter and chaos. Skip those projects that you're not interested in and add your own suggestions as needed.

Oh, No! It's That Time Again!

1ST STEP: THE SUNDAY SETUP
(TAKE 10 MINUTES)

- Check your calendar and be sure all appointments and meetings are listed.

✐ Add reminders of things to do on your calendar.

✐ Check your PRIORITY LIST and decide on projects and special tasks that need to be done.

TIPS: Consider using the Just Do It tip to prepare the Sunday Setup; Multitask and watch a ballgame while checking your PRIORITY LIST; and Take a 10-Minute Computer or Project Break to set up your weekly medication.

2ND STEP: GET THE GOOD HOUSEKEEPING AWARD (TAKE 1 TO 2 HOURS)

✐ Quickly straighten each room by stacking mail, magazines, newspapers, and CDs, by arranging pillows, by gathering up toys, and by hanging up clothes.

✐ Water plants and collect trash from each room.

✐ Put newspapers, catalogs, cans, and bottles in the recycling bins.

✐ Tidy the kitchen, counter, stove, and table as needed.

✐ Straighten up the bathroom counter.

✐ Clean the toilet, bathtub, mirrors, counter, and sink.

✐ Once everything is picked up and cleaned, sweep the floors.

✐ Dust and vacuum each room.

TIPS: Consider using the Couch Potatoes Arise tip to clean during commercials; Half-and-Half to clean the main floor one day and the upstairs another day; Just Do It and clean the whole house on Saturday morning; Outsource and hire someone to clean twice a month; and Share the Fun by assigning chores to family members.

3RD STEP: TWEAKING TIME (TAKE 30 MINUTES TO 1 HOUR)

✐ Zip around and do some quick household fix-ups and problem solving, such as adding new batteries, or do a little paint touch-up by the stairs.

✐ Organize your purse, wallet, tote bag, or briefcase.

✐ Sort and file any new photographs.

TIPS: Consider using the Couch Potatoes Arise tip to change a lightbulb; Just Do It and tackle a painting project; Multitask and sort new photos while watching a TV program; and Take a 10-Minute Computer or Project Break to organize your purse or to file a few CDs and DVDs.

4TH STEP: LAUNDRY CYCLE (TAKE 1 TO 2 HOURS)

✐ Gather up then wash and dry clothes.

✐ Sort, fold, and put away clean clothes.

✐ Iron clothes, sew on buttons, or repair items.

TIPS: Consider using the Couch Potatoes Arise tip and toss in a load of laundry during a commercial; Half-and-Half to iron half the clothes one day and the rest the following day; Multitask and iron or mend clothes while watching a talk show; Share the Fun and have the kids do the laundry; and Take a 10-Minute Computer or Project Break to zip up and down the stairs to switch the clothes from the washer to the dryer.

5TH STEP: THE GREAT OUTDOORS (TAKE 15 TO 30 MINUTES)

✐ Sweep the porch, deck, and sidewalk.

✐ Pick up toys, trash, and dog deposits.

✐ Water the grass and plants.

✐ Take out the trash from your vehicles.

✐ Bring any papers, receipts, and clothes into the house.

✐ Get gasoline and wash your vehicles as needed.

TIPS: Consider using the Divide and Conquer tip for big gardening projects; Half-and-Half to mow the front yard one day and the back another day; Just Do It and clean your car; Outsource and hire someone to shovel snow and mow the lawn; and Share the Fun by getting the kids to rake up the leaves.

6TH STEP: PLOW THROUGH THE PAPERWORK (TAKE 30 MINUTES TO 1 HOUR)

✐ Pay bills and deal with important business papers.

✐ Balance your checkbook.

✐ Respond to personal letters and send cards.

✐ Place receipts and business papers in the TO BE FILED folder.

✐ Sort through miscellaneous articles and pamphlets. Either throw them away or file them into your GENERAL INFORMATION and ACTION folders or into your PERSONAL INTEREST folders.

✐ Place old magazines, newspapers, and catalogs in the recycling bins.

✐ File business papers at least once a month in your permanent folders.

TIPS: Consider using the Half-and-Half tip and pay bills one day and handle business papers and personal letters another day; Just Do It and write cards and letters one evening; Multitask and clip articles to save while watching the news; and Share the Fun so that when you pay the bills your spouse will file all the papers.

Are you still wondering whether the DAILY and WEEKLY ROUTINES might be more trouble than they're worth? Let's look at an example of how a routine can help.

My niece just had premature twins. She was in the hospital for seven days. That meant that her husband was home, alone, for a whole week. Now I don't actually know what happened, but let's just say that her husband let things go. After all, he had a perfect excuse. He was working, his wife was in the hospital, and he was worrying about the babies.

Here's how easy it is for clutter to take over:

✐ On the first day of clutter, he left the mail on the kitchen counter.

✐ On the second day of clutter, he put the mail on the sofa and a mug of coffee on the coffee table.

✐ On the third day, the mail ended up on the dining room table, there's a new bag of chips on the sofa, and a jacket is thrown over the chair.

✐ On the fourth day, the mail is by the computer, there's a book on the piano, a fast food bag on the ottoman, and a towel on the bathroom floor.

✐ On the fifth day, the mail is on a bookshelf, pajamas are on the floor, toothpaste is on the counter, a can of pop is on an end table, and gym shoes are in the middle of the living room.

It only gets worse. By the end of the seventh day, he's got a clear case of clutter and his wife is coming home the next day. He has two choices and they're both bad. He can race around for a couple of hours cleaning up, and who wants to do that, or he can say, "Hey, sorry it's a mess, but I just couldn't get around to cleaning." In that case, my niece comes home to face a monster mess.

This could have been avoided if he had decided to follow the DAILY ROUTINE. Each day, all he had to do was take a couple of minutes to pick up after himself in the bathroom and bedroom, and take a few more minutes to put the food away, and slip the dishes into the dishwasher. It wouldn't take long to quickly sort the mail, to answer only the most important phone messages and e-mail, and to pop a load of clothes into the washer. He doesn't have to vacuum or wash the floor, just follow some simple routines, and not create any clutter.

By following the DAILY ROUTINE, my niece's husband could have worked, spent time at the hospital, and then come back to a reasonably neat house. He could have that uncluttered home with only a little bit of effort each day—thanks to the DAILY ROUTINE.

Chapter 23

THE YEARLY CHECKLIST

∿∿∿∿∿∿∿∿∿∿∿∿∿∿∿∿∿

Help!

It's April 15. Are you one of those people we see on TV waiting in line to mail their income taxes just before the midnight deadline? Does the whole tax thing kind of creep up on you? Are you always playing catch-up with routine household projects that you know will come around every year? Can you do something about it? Yup! Maybe it's time to use this YEARLY CHECKLIST. Here's the plan.

The First Part of the Plan Is *Schedule It*

Don't panic! No one expects you to do everything on this list. It's just a guide to help you keep track of all those clutter culprits and of what needs to be done and to remind you that it's time to do it. For example:

- Each Sunday while you're setting up your plans for the week, choose a priority project, such as cleaning out the garage.
- Look at your calendar and set up an hour after work on Monday to start pulling out items in the garage to be dumped or recycled,

Friday after dinner sort the gardening items, and finish up the garage on Saturday.

The Next Part of the Plan Is *Organize It*

The following monthly steps will help you control your clutter.

The Yearly Checklist

Use this month-by-month checklist to help you decide your priority projects and responsibilities. Skip any ideas that don't apply to you and add your own suggestions as needed.

January

CALENDAR CHECK

- Set up a calendar for the entire year. Add birthdays, anniversaries, and special occasions for each month.
- What meetings, social engagements, and medical or hair appointments are scheduled for this month? Add them to the calendar.

TO DO

- Put away all holiday decorations and new gifts.
- Check Christmas card envelopes and update your address book.
- Start a new folder for all tax information that begins coming in.
- If needed, set up new folders and envelopes for business papers for the coming year.
- Every year go through all the file cabinets:
  - Remove outdated materials
  - Make folders for new materials
  - Reorganize the folders as necessary

February

CALENDAR CHECK

- Are there any birthdays, anniversaries, and special occasions?
- Are there any meetings and appointments?

TO DO

- Start gathering up tax information.
- Pay winter taxes.
- Make spring vacation plans.

March

CALENDAR CHECK

- Are there any birthdays, anniversaries, and special occasions?
- Are there any meetings and appointments?

TO DO

- Finish state and federal taxes.
- Make Easter plans.

April

CALENDAR CHECK

- Are there any birthdays, anniversaries, and special occasions?
- Are there any meetings and appointments?

TO DO

- Don't forget to get your taxes in on time.
- Clean and put away winter equipment, such as the snow blower.
- Look over your spring and summer clothes. Decide what you can remove from your collection and what items you need to buy.

✐ Sort winter clothes, donate some, and clean and store the rest.

✐ Start vacation planning for the summer.

May

CALENDAR CHECK

✐ Are there any birthdays, anniversaries, and special occasions?

✐ Are there any meetings and appointments?

TO DO

✐ Make plans for Mother's Day.

✐ Make plans for a graduation party.

✐ Start spring gardening and yard work:

- Rake, weed, and trim.
- Buy topsoil, fertilizer, grass seed, and flowers to plant.
- Add topsoil and fertilizer.
- Plant flowers and grass seed.
- Put out garden hoses, patio furniture, and the grill.
- Put gas in the lawn mower.

✐ Start basement, attic, and garage spring cleaning:

- Try to do a major check once a year.
- Fix up the laundry area, exercise area, or any of the other special areas.
- Check each box and shelf to see if you're storing a bunch of stuff you don't even want anymore.
- Straighten and organize the shelves as necessary.
- Dust, sweep, wash, and vacuum.

✐ Start bathroom spring cleaning:

- Every once in awhile check the bathroom and linen closet for over-loaded and messy drawers and shelves.
- Sort through everything and pull out items you don't need; be sure the remaining items are neat, organized, and ready for use.
- Dust, sweep, wash, and vacuum.

✐ Start bedroom spring cleaning:

- Rotate your mattresses several times a year.

- At the end of each season pull out clothes and accessories that you really don't need anymore.
- Things can get a little messy when you're in a hurry; straighten your closets, dresser drawers, and jewelry box.
- Whenever you add new clothes and accessories, consider taking out some of your older things to give away.
- Before you switch to your summer or winter wardrobe, remove anything that just doesn't make you look your best.
- Dust, sweep, wash, and vacuum.

Start foyer, living room, family room, and dining room spring cleaning:

- Wax the furniture.
- Dust lamp shades and the tops of pictures and mirrors.
- Clean the phones, TV, and computer screens.
- Wash areas around light switches and doorknobs.
- Vacuum the curtains and upholstery.
- Wash and wax the floors.
- Wash the windows.
- Wash the carpet and throw rugs.
- Clean the fireplace.
- Add potting soil and fertilizer to house plants.
- Clean plant leaves.

Start kitchen spring cleaning:

- Every year or two empty each cupboard and clean it with a damp sponge; wash the glasses and dishes; do a quick sort and reorganize as you put everything back.
- Pull out the refrigerator and stove; wash the top, front, back, and sides of each; clean the floor before pushing them back.
- Every once in awhile spiffy up the place by washing the cupboard doors and then waxing them.
- Sift through your recipe envelope or box of recipes that you've never tried; be realistic and dump as many as you can.

June

CALENDAR CHECK

Are there any birthdays, anniversaries, and special occasions?

Are there any meetings and appointments?

TO DO

- Make plans for Father's Day.
- Make plans for the Fourth of July.
- Finish gardening and yard projects.

July

CALENDAR CHECK

- Are there any birthdays, anniversaries, and special occasions?
- Are there any meetings and appointments?

TO DO

- Maintain the garden and yard.
- Pay summer taxes.

August

CALENDAR CHECK

- Are there any birthdays, anniversaries, and special occasions?
- Are there any meetings and appointments?

TO DO

- Maintain the garden and yard.
- Buy back-to-school clothes and supplies.
- Set up a folder for important school information.

September

CALENDAR CHECK

- Are there any birthdays, anniversaries, and special occasions?
- Are there any meetings and appointments?

TO DO

- Clean out the garage so that you can get the car in this winter.
- Start a gift list with ideas for Christmas.

October

CALENDAR CHECK

- Are there any birthdays, anniversaries, and special occasions?
- Are there any meetings and appointments?

TO DO

- Make decisions about Halloween costumes, candy, and decorations.
- Start winterizing:
  - Weed and trim plants.
  - Rake the leaves.
  - Clean out the gutters.
  - Clean and put away garden hoses, patio furniture, and the grill.
  - Wash the windows.
  - Get out shovels and the snow blower.
  - Clean and close the pool.
  - Take the car in for a tune-up, check the tires, and add wiper fluid.
  - Be sure you have an extra blanket, tools, window scraper, flashlight, and bag of sand in the car.
  - Restock your pantry with plenty of extra canned goods, pet food and pet supplies, toilet paper, tissues, laundry products, cleaning supplies, health items, bottles of water, and flashlight batteries.
- Buy Christmas or season's greetings cards and look for gifts.
- Decide on general plans for Thanksgiving, Christmas, Hanukkah, Kwanzaa, and New Year's Eve.

November

CALENDAR CHECK

- Are there any birthdays, anniversaries, and special occasions?
- Are there any meetings and appointments?

TO DO

- Finish any outdoor winterizing:
  - Rake leaves one last time.
  - Mow the lawn, empty the gasoline tank, and clean and store the lawn mower.

🖎 Get ready for Thanksgiving.

🖎 Work on holiday cards and gift buying.

December

CALENDAR CHECK

🖎 Are there any birthdays, anniversaries, and special occasions?

🖎 Are there any meetings and appointments?

TO DO

🖎 Start making holiday plans:
  • Put up seasonal decorations.
  • Put up outside decorations.
  • Mail cards.
  • Wrap and mail gifts.
  • Wrap the rest of your gifts.
  • Bake holiday treats.
  • Make plans for special holiday concerts, plays, and religious programs.
  • Finish plans for special days of the holiday season.

What's the Final Step?

Use the YEARLY CHECKLIST to help you plan ahead and avoid lots of last-minute running around. Now it's time to *Set Up a Routine to Control Clutter and Chaos*.

WEEKLY: Take 10 to 15 Minutes to Set Up New Projects

❏ During your Sunday Setup, check the YEARLY CHECKLIST and schedule your next project.

❑ Add new projects to the list and ignore things that don't apply to your household.

❑ Don't forget the Tips List discussed in Chapter 22 for tackling big projects:

- Couch Potatoes Arise
- Divide and Conquer
- Half-and-Half
- Just Do It
- Multitask
- Outsource
- Share the Fun
- Take a 10-Minute Computer or Project Break

INDEX

ABOUT THE AUTHOR

Joyce really doesn't spend her days and evenings cleaning and organizing. She has traveled around the world, earned a black belt in karate, and played tennis and softball, until her knees gave out.

She was a public school librarian/media specialist. After retiring, she has followed her own advice, and handles cleaning and organizing projects as quickly and efficiently as possible. Then she has time to do all the things she really enjoys such as reading mysteries, playing the piano, taking photographs, traveling, writing, and going to lunch or dinner and a movie with friends.